Praise for *The Pink Tax*

"*The Pink Tax* is a terrific book. Janine Rogan offers punchy advice for patriarchy-proofing your finances, and for how financial institutions can get behind this movement."
SARAH KAPLAN, director of the Institute for Gender and the Economy at the University of Toronto's Rotman School of Management

"*The Pink Tax* is a must-read for anyone who's sick of gendered policies, prices, and societal expectations, and who is ready to fight for financial feminism through their daily actions. Janine Rogan takes a pointed look at how women get the short end of the stick in everything from annual raises to interest rates, and what we can do to combat it and build our wealth."
ERIN BURY, cofounder and CEO of Willful

"*The Pink Tax* is full of real-world examples and stats to back up the high cost of being a marginalized gender identity in our society. Not only is a strong case made for the impacts of societal, systemic, and generational trauma that women experience, Janine Rogan also presents a vision with action steps to help us reimagine capitalism."
CHANTEL CHAPMAN, cofounder and CEO of Trauma of Money

"Janine Rogan masterfully unravels the patriarchal systems holding women back and provides actionable steps to fight back. *The Pink Tax* is a must-read for women at every age and stage."
KERRY K. TAYLOR, founder of Squawkfox

"*The Pink Tax* shines a light on the obstacles women face when it comes to managing their money!"

SHANNON LEE SIMMONS, CFP, CIM, and founder of the New School of Finance

"Janine Rogan shows us a clear road map to achieve a financially equal society. Her facts about the Pink Tax will shock you and motivate you to rise up, be in control of your finances, and help other women and girls do the same."

LESLEY-ANNE SCORGIE, founder of MeVest

"Gender inequalities are very real and go beyond the financial world. Janine Rogan tackles the issues directly by demanding financial equality, highlighting how building wealth is in fact self-care. This book leaves you feeling empowered and dares you to become part of the solution. Loved it."

PATTIE LOVETT-REID, former chief financial commentator at CTV News

"An absolute game changer for those left out of the conversation."

SIM & SONYA, founders of Girls That Invest

"*The Pink Tax* should be required reading for any woman aiming to take control of her personal finances. In this well-sourced book, Janine Rogan exposes the challenges women face when it comes to patriarchal financial systems, but offers exciting solutions that leave you feeling empowered about your financial choices. Janine is your personal finance champion!"

ANGELA OSBORNE, c/o The Jilly Academy

THE PINK TAX

Dismantling a Financial
System Designed to
Keep **Women** Broke

THE PINK TAX

JANINE ROGAN CPA

●● PAGE TWO

Cataloguing in publication information is available
from Library and Archives Canada.
ISBN 978-1-77458-370-8 (paperback)
ISBN 978-1-77458-371-5 (ebook)

Page Two
pagetwo.com

Edited by Kendra Ward
Copyedited by Crissy Calhoun
Proofread by Alison Strobel
Cover design by Taysia Louie
Cover illustration by Peter Cocking
Interior design and illustrations by Taysia Louie

pinktaxbook.com

Theodore, may you grow up in a world where
every man is as strong a feminist as your father is.
You are my everything.

Andrew, I love you more than any words
I'll ever be able to write.

CONTENTS

"The truth will
set you free but first
it will piss you off."

GLORIA STEINEM

GOT THE
PINK TAX BLUES?

O NE OF my first money memories is of starting a lemonade stand one hot summer Sunday with two other kids from down the street, a pair of sweet young boys whom I corralled into business with me. Together, we mixed the lemonade, made a sign, and put up the stand, charging a cool loonie (one Canadian dollar) per thirst-quenching cup. Business was brisk that day, and by the time we had sold all the lemonade, we had in its place a respectable bowl full of our neighbors' loose change. It was time to divvy up the proceeds of the day's sales.

That's when I pretended to not understand the difference between a loonie and a quarter. After convincing the two boys that all the coins were of equal value, I divided all the coins equally among us—making sure that most of the loonies were in my pile. My father later audited my split of the proceeds and proceeded to educate us all about the different value of the coins—something he knew I was already keenly aware of. He took me aside and spoke to me about the importance of honesty and integrity. Suitably shamed, I have never tried to hoodwink anyone again.

Perhaps from an early age, I was already fighting the patriarchy. When I was a little girl, I was told that I could be anything I wanted. But if this is so, why is it that, even today, white women in the US make only 83 cents for every dollar men earn?[1] The truth is that because I was born with two X chromosomes, achieving... well, really, anything is more challenging. So it could be that even as a little girl, I realized that having more money was an advantage. Money is a tool that allows you to live a certain life, and while it's not the be all and end all, it sure makes life easier if you have it.

Because I am an assertive woman who takes charge of her life, I've been told I am bossy, pissy, bitchy, controlling, emotional, loud, and angry—all of which are considered extremely negative traits for a woman. I can't help but wonder if men are ever called these things or if they are applauded for their leadership skills, confidence, and their passion. I think Taylor Swift has it right: I probably would get there quicker if I were man.

When I consider the injustices in my own life, I think of promotions I've been passed over for, instances I've been talked over, moments I've been dismissed, times I've been discounted for being too young, and words that I've been called for speaking my mind. So often we separate sexist behavior and the impact it has on our bank accounts. But these two things are intertwined, and it's time we understand their connection.

If you've heard of the Pink Tax, it was probably in the context of the price discrepancy between products and services that are marketed toward women versus nearly identical ones targeted to men.[2] Walk into any drugstore or grocery store, and you'll quickly see that the women's product is more expensive, or if it's the same price as the man's, the amount of product is substantially smaller. At my grocery store in downtown Calgary, the Pink Tax is rampant:

- Gillette razor (top of the line): women's $21.99; men's $15.99

- Gillette shaving cream: women's $1.86/100g; men's $1.76/100g

- Dove shampoo (same volume): women's $4.48; men's $3.99

These are just three simple and easily found examples, but the Pink Tax is so much more sinister than this. It extends into the very fabric of our society, and it costs women a lot over the course of their lives.

I've seen pink-branded calculators, earplugs, kid's helmets, and clothing that cost more—it's everywhere. Although it may seem like a few dollars and cents don't make a big difference, it adds up. The Pink Tax costs women $82,000 by the time they are sixty,[3] and that figure only includes the things the researchers were measuring. In a 1995 study in the *American Economic Review*, researchers documented the initial prices women and men were offered at car dealerships. On average, white women were quoted $200 more than their white male counterparts, and Black women were quoted $400 more.[4] In today's dollars, those numbers double—meaning Black women are quoted $800 more on average.

But the Pink Tax is about more than what we pay for the things we purchase daily, weekly, annually, and over a lifetime. It is about our jobs, our investments, and our families. The Pink Tax is the price we pay for being who we are in a world designed to keep women broke.

At work, for example, being spoken over is an area that women tend to have domain expertise. This sometimes results in us not putting our ideas forward, which might mean we're not respected as much as male colleagues. When it comes time for promotions and raises, the impact of always being spoken over results in a negative financial impact in our lives.

The overturn of *Roe v. Wade* in the US makes it a tumultuous time to be a woman. If we can't control what happens to our bodies and don't have access to the basic human right of health care, how are we supposed to control what happens to our bank accounts? And even where abortion care is legal and accessible, often it is women who pay for abortions as well as for the travel costs and time associated with having this procedure.

The patriarchy runs deep.

What is the patriarchy?

The *International Encyclopedia of Human Geography* defines *patriarchy* as "a system of relationships, beliefs, and values embedded in political, social, and economic systems that structure gender inequality between men and women. Attributes seen as 'feminine' or pertaining to women are undervalued, while attributes regarded as 'masculine' or pertaining to men are celebrated."[5]

Though you may not always notice them, there are examples of how deep the patriarchy runs in our everyday life. Our society values paid corporate jobs over unpaid care work. The C-suite is dominated by white men. The patriarchy is evident across all media forms—TV shows, movies, and advertising—and when we look at our bank accounts. It's time for change.

I wrote this book to address what's happening in our society from a financial perspective and to challenge how the systems that have been perpetuated over hundreds of years impact women's bank accounts. For the past twelve years, I've been passionate about educating millennial and Gen Z women about their finances. This book is the culmination of my research and the biases I've uncovered when it comes to women building wealth. While my aim is always to be inclusive, there is not much research to support analysis beyond the gender binary. Because of the lack of data, this book is predominantly focused on cis women. This is a good reminder for me and everyone that we need to collect data as inclusively as possible so we can continue to uncover and solve the issues that all women face.

This isn't your typical personal finance book. My hope is that as you read it, your eyes will be opened to how unjust our financial system is and to the many systemic barriers and pressures women face—at no fault of our own. I'm sick of old white men telling women to just save more money by

skipping the shoe purchase or the latte, without accounting for the fact that the entire financial system was set up
by men to benefit men. That makes it hard for women to
get the education and support they may need to address
what's working against them. This book will also give you
practical, real-world tips for building wealth and actionable
steps to improve your financial situation, whatever it might
be. We'll also be talking about the challenges and adversity
we as women face when it comes to managing our money.
By the end of it all, you'll see the biases working against us
and be ready to act to make our financial system more fair.

The four foundations of financial feminism

Feminism often gets a bad reputation, but I want to clear up
what *feminism* actually means.

Feminism is the advocacy of women's rights on the
basis of the equality of the sexes.[6]

Read that again—and focus on the *equality* part.

That's it. That's all you need to know. *Feminism is the
equality of the sexes*. It's not man-hating or eliminating
men—and all genders can certainly be feminists.

Feminism is equality for all.

Financial feminism is the advocacy of financial equity
across genders.[7] Throughout history, women have been
subject to inequality. White women legally gained the right
to vote in Canada in 1918.[8] In the US, they couldn't own
their own credit cards[9] or qualify for a mortgage indepen-

dently until 1974.[10] More marginalized groups of women faced greater barriers and slower timelines. In Canada, Inuit people were granted the right to vote in 1950[11] and First Nations in 1960.[12] In the US, Asian Americans gained the right to vote in 1952, thirty-two years after white women.[13] Advocacy for women's rights hasn't always included all women—sometimes feminism actually means white feminism.

Injustice and inequity in society do not result from one specific law or structure but rather are the product of the system as a whole. We have been raised in a patriarchal society with practices and rules that have been outlined predominantly by white men, for centuries. The answer to inequity isn't simple; it's extremely complex. Inequalities are baked into the very fabric of our society and will take years of advocacy, political will, and policy changes to undo.

If we continue on without seriously addressing the financial discrimination against women, a 2020 World Economic Forum[14] report suggests we will not have equal economic participation until the year 2277—that's more than 250 years! I don't know about you, but the fact that my grandchildren are unlikely to experience economic gender parity is extremely troubling, to put it lightly. If we follow the trajectory we are on now, my great-great-great-great-grandchildren will be among the first generation to see the closing of the gender pay gap. As a society we must move faster than this.

Women are just as capable as anyone else in the realm of financial literacy, but in many cases we lack the confidence to take the first step to learn. A "head in the sand" approach about money is ingrained in us, and many women have been conditioned to hand over their important financial decisions to others.

Financial feminism extends beyond the individual to address the societal inequities that are deeply rooted in our culture. Money shouldn't be a taboo topic, and women shouldn't be afraid to talk about it. We are not greedy or bitchy or obnoxious for wanting to own our financial future. Frankly, anyone who thinks that is part of the problem.

The work I've done in the financial space over the last decade has allowed me to identify the challenges women face when managing their money. I don't have all the solutions, but I have identified four active principles—the four foundations of financial feminism—that will help women achieve financial equality faster.

1 **Demand financial equality.** The system is set up to disadvantage and disempower women when it comes to our finances. We will look at how important it is to be involved in building our financial futures.

2 **Build wealth for self-care.** We must start to look at financial self-care as part of the holistic definition and experience of self-care.

3 **Support new moms.** Whether or not a woman has children, we will never get to financial equality in our society if we don't find a way to better support new moms. Financially speaking, one of the worst decisions a woman can make is to have a child. We need to change that.

4 **Vote for your daughters.** Often people tell me that personal finance isn't or shouldn't be political, but the truth is until we stop making laws around women and their bodies, money is and will continue to be political.

When women flourish, all of society benefits. These four crucial principles boil down the individual and global actions that our communities, our countries, and our world need. My hope is that you learn about them in this book and then take them with you as you continue on your journey to financial independence.

On voting and public policy

If you haven't figured it out by now, my political bias leans left. Political opinions are often left out of money conversations, but the realm of politics is paramount to gaining equity. As we have all experienced with the COVID-19 pandemic, money is political. When it comes to advocating for universal basic income, helping low-income individuals access benefits they are entitled to, or managing budget cuts that predominantly affect women's health, who we vote for largely affects our finances.

Because I have my Chartered Professional Accountant (CPA) designation, many people assume that I am conservative, voting for lower taxes and "putting business first." But these kinds of policies are a mistake on all fronts. Assisting and providing for the lowest-income earners and most vulnerable people in our society elevates all of society and collectively saves us money.[15] From decreased health care costs to fewer opioid-related deaths, increasing social spending is a good thing for society and advances equality. All this to say, you can be smart with money and vote progressively at the same time.

The myth of meritocracy

In 1958 the term *meritocracy* was coined by Michael Young, a British sociologist. Meritocracy is defined as the holding of power by people selected on the basis of their abilities.[16] Young warned that a system that rewarded merit could actually lead to a dystopian society where the "losers" suffered more than ever.[17]

Today, more often than not, we hear of merit awards and promotions being a good thing—they worked hard, so they deserve it.

But that couldn't be further from the truth.

If we unpack what a meritocracy actually looks like, it is completely problematic. Whether or not someone has "merit" is decided by individuals who have already acquired merit. And people are biased about who they choose to be rewarded for their hard work. For example, if a company executive team is made up of older white men with no responsibilities at home, are they going to see a single working mother as someone who has equal or greater merit than them? The answer is no, it would seem; admittance into the elite few is still biased in favor of those who share the same identities as the existing elite.[18]

Snowball inequality,[19] a phenomenon described by Daniel Markovits, allows elite workers to acquire super-skilled jobs that ultimately displace middle-class laborers. The elite workers then use their abundance of wealth to ensure they can educate their children at prestigious universities and continue to monopolize high-skilled industries, as compared to their middle-class counterparts. This continues to suppress the lower and middle classes; regardless of how hard they work, they just can't get ahead.

We must address the mistaken idea that if people "just worked harder," they would achieve the American dream and build millions (or billions) in wealth. This simply isn't true. Anyone who says they just "want to hire the best person for the job" (a phrase I've heard *way* too often) is lazy. Of course we all want to hire qualified and competent candidates, but in my experience this type of language is used as a cop-out for not hiring people who don't look like, talk like, or have a similar background to the hiring manager.

Taking financial control

Despite my early adventures in the lemonade-stand business, by the time I was nineteen years old, I really didn't know a whole lot about money, other than how to spend it. I was working a full-time summer job, earning between $19 and $21 an hour, and at the end of the season had $10 in my bank account. I had nothing to show for all my hard work. Cue the shame and embarrassment. I knew I had to take control of my finances. I started to consider why I didn't know much about money and how to manage it. When I looked around, I saw this was true for other women too.

Now I am the first to admit the privilege I have. I'm a white, able-bodied, heterosexual, cisgender woman who was raised by upper-middle-class parents. Said parents paid for my university and helped my husband and me purchase our first home, just like their parents did for them. Although I have been afforded many privileges, it is glaringly obvious to me how broken our financial system is—and that's what I want to address. For all women to "get out from under," we each need to develop our financial literacy and to demand societal changes for the greater good. In these pages, I'm going to show you that it's possible to build your wealth and fix the system at the same time.

I eventually became a CPA, and I married one as well. My husband and I talked about money early on in our relationship and started tracking our net worth when we moved in together in 2012. Back then, we had a combined net worth of $17,000. A decade later, at ages thirty-one (me) and thirty-six (him), we have more than half a million dollars to our names. I've personally grown my wealth to the point that I no longer need to contribute on an annual basis to my investments for them to grow. Knowing we will be okay financially is a freeing feeling. Sure, we have had ups and downs. In the past decade, we have had four periods when one of us wasn't working, but because we had built a solid financial foundation, our net worth still grew in those periods even though we weren't adding anything to our savings.

I want this kind of security for you too, dear reader. I've spent my career thus far understanding finances, whether for businesses or individuals, and my mission has always been to educate the public about their money. After working for a software company, I've seen firsthand how much technology can do for us. Understanding what tools to explore and implement allows you to see your finances in a different light, and it ultimately makes your finances easier to approach and understand. Taking care of your financial house is so important and will set you up for success in the long term. And I'm here to show you how to do so.

In addition to the personal side of personal finance, I'm here to empower you to help fix the system. There are things we can all do to build a future that serves every one of us financially. Women's financial well-being benefits our entire society by building economic growth and keeping those that are most at risk out of poverty.[20]

So let's smash the Pink Tax together.

Welcome financial feminists, I'm so glad you are here.

PART

1

Demand Financial Equality

"What is the greatest lesson a woman should learn? That since day one she's already had everything she needs within herself."

RUPI KAUR

WOMEN HAVE long been deterred from building wealth. It really wasn't that long ago that women couldn't have their own bank accounts, credit cards, or property. Women were considered property of their fathers until they were married and then they became property of their husbands, so there really was "no need" for them to build their own wealth. In the US, it wasn't until 1963 that employers were required to pay women equally for jobs that entailed the same skill, effort, and responsibility and 1966 when employers could not deny promotions on the basis of sex.[1]

This wealth gap between men and women—which is in part perpetuated by the social norm that women shouldn't talk about money—is evident in the statistics. Even women in the top 1 percent have disproportionately lower incomes than their male counterparts, earning on average $362,000 per year while men in the top 1 percent earn $392,000. The wealth gap goes all the way to the top.[2]

The disproportion of wealth makes women reliant on men as a financial resource, but we can end this vicious cycle by earning and building our wealth. We must demand financial equality for ourselves, for other women, and from institutions. This is one of the best ways we can fight the patriarchy.

1

THROUGH
A NEW LENS

HOW WOULD it feel if you could pay for postsecondary tuition and your living expenses for the year with one summer of full-time work? Oh, and you'd still have some money left over for beer.

If you're thinking, *That isn't a big deal,* you are probably a baby boomer (born between 1946 and 1964). But if you are thinking, *Wow, that would be amazing—and it's totally unrealistic,* then you're probably a millennial like me (born between 1981 and 1996) or a part of Gen Z (born between 1996 and 2012).

Today's twenty- and thirty-somethings face unique circumstances when it comes to building their wealth and securing financial independence. Five main factors increase financial instability for younger generations:

1   **Inflated postsecondary costs.** The cost of postsecondary has soared astronomically in the last several decades. Students graduate with more and more debt,

which makes it harder for them to build wealth in the early years of their postgraduation life.

2   **The housing crisis.** We have seen a drastic uptick in the cost of entering the housing market with the prices of homes at all time high here in Canada.

3   **Wage stagnation.** Accounting for inflation, the average worker's wages have not significantly increased since the 1970s and have even decreased in some situations. With the cost of everyday goods and services on the rise, it is harder to afford basic needs. In 2022, inflation in Canada rose up to 7.7 percent,[1] which is a ten-year high.

4   **The wage gap.** Because women still earn less on the dollar than men, women have less disposable income and less savings than our male counterparts. Beyond women receiving less pay for the same work as men, the wage gap also includes detrimental factors such as women being passed over for promotions and women working in less lucrative industries. This also impacts men, who may have greater financial responsibility in heterosexual partnerships.

5   **Childcare costs.** Thankfully, we are seeing a move toward affordable, accessible childcare in Canada, but there is still so much work to do. Post-pandemic, the average cost of childcare has increased by 41 percent[2] in the US. In Canada, it costs an average of $45 per day[3] for infants under eighteen months (approximately $1,000 per month, but this number varies by province). With childcare costs eating up more than 10 percent of

a family's income (and sometimes up to 30 percent), it can be extremely challenging for families to manage, let alone make extra mortgage payments, invest, save for their children's postsecondary, or save for retirement.

These five factors have caused our generational wealth to plummet.

The world today is different than it was for our parents' generation. A lot has changed economically, financially, politically, and socially. It is impossible for millennials and Gen Z to have the same financial experiences as their parents' had.

The circumstances we are born into play a large role in how financially successful we are later in life. My life would be a lot different if I had been born in a developing country to parents who could barely afford to feed us. That's the whole point about privilege: it is unearned. And if we are going to move toward equality for all, everyone needs to identify and own the privilege they have. In my case, I was born into circumstances that have benefited me throughout my life. My children will be in a similar situation, and that's how generational privilege is perpetuated. Understanding our advantages is key to identifying the gaps experienced by others, by virtue of circumstances they too had no control over.

My mom and I have had very similar experiences in our professional lives. We both attended the University of Alberta and earned accounting degrees, hers in 1982 and mine in 2014. Both of us articled at the same Big Four accounting firm and she even "introduced me into the profession" once I received my designation—the same thing her father did for her. You could say that the apple doesn't fall far from the tree. And yet the world was a much different place for her than it was for me.

In 1982, university tuition cost my mom $1,200 per year (around $3,400 in 2023 dollars). My business degree was closer to $8,000 per year—more than twice the amount.

Today in Canada, the average student debtor owes about $43,000 to $48,000,[4] which includes student loans, lines of credit, and personal loans. Average salaries of university graduates start at $54,000 a year.

My mom's starting salary was $18,000, which is generous when you compare it to the price of my parents' first home: $100,000, or roughly five times her starting salary.

My starting salary, thirty years later at the exact same company, was a bit more than double hers: $41,000. But the cost of our first home was vastly different: it cost my husband and me $600,000. That's fourteen times(!!) my starting salary.

In 2021, the cost of housing skyrocketed, with the average Canadian house price sitting at just over $711,000.[5] That's fourteen times the average new graduate's starting salary. As interest rates increase over the next few years, prices may decline but not nearly to the level of five times a new graduate's starting salary (or $270,000).

The baby boomer generation could amass wealth in different ways and more quickly. Boomers secured their first homes for a fraction of the price of homes today. University tuition and living expenses could easily be covered with a summer job, and starting salaries were generous compared to the cost of living.

We can't live up to the financial standards or lifestyles of our parents. **But we can flip the narrative about how to build wealth.**

Millennials and Gen Z face unprecedented financial hurdles to amassing any kind of wealth. To pay for one year of tuition, students today need to work three times more hours at a minimum wage job than students did in the late 1970s and early 1980s. Between classes, homework, and volunteer requirements, there is little time left to work, let alone to work three times the hours that our parents did, in hopes of graduating debt-free.

Unpacking the wealth gap between generations is complex, but nevertheless it is important to consider. One of the main drivers of the generational wealth gap is stagnant wages. Wages have stagnated and even decreased over the past forty years, but productivity is at an all-time high—it has gone up 299 percent in the last fifty years,[6] and yet we aren't working any less or being paid any more. The wage gap between men and women compounds the problem. American women earn just 83 cents[7] for every dollar men earn, and when a woman's race, class, or sexual orientation, for example, are factored in, the gap gets even wider, with women of color earning just 61 cents[8] for every dollar a man earns.

These economic factors are multiplied by the popular notion that we can all become "self-made"; in other words, we shouldn't need to accept any outside help to elevate ourselves in society. We just need to work harder and pull ourselves up by the bootstraps. The expression "to pull yourself up by the bootstraps" was coined in the nineteenth century to describe something absurd—to pull yourself up by the strap of your boot is impossible. It wasn't until a full century later that this phrase started to be used as a metaphor for self-improvement. So let's consider this: when society tells young people to pull themselves up by the bootstraps—that all they need to do is to work harder, to stop being so lazy or entitled—it is asking for the absurd.

What happens if you don't have any boots? Or your boots are stuck in the mud? Or your boots aren't as big as the person sitting next to you?

How do you pull yourself up to a comparable lifestyle as the generations before you? Or to have a better life than your parents had?

When the baby boomers were in their twenties and thirties, they held 21 percent of the wealth in the US, compared to the 6.6 percent[9] millennials hold today.[10] In 1989, boomers with college debt had a net wealth of $86,500. A quarter century later, millennials' net wealth is a dismal $6,600.

My point isn't about who had it harder—it isn't a competition—but to show you how different it is for today's generations and to empower you to earn wealth a different way. In the '70s, '80s, and even part of the '90s, an entire household could be supported by one income (depending, of course, on the level of income). Many women worked in the home (and not in the work-from-home context we're in today). This wasn't necessarily a good thing for financial advancement. But many families could live comfortably on a single income, and in many families, the person who was working (often the man) had a pension to carry them and their spouse through retirement. Today we rarely have that option—it feels impossible to have only one income to support an average family, and hardly any twenty- and thirty-somethings have pensions. If they do have a pension, they likely have a *defined contribution pension* (which employees mainly fund and employers match; the pension is paid out until it is gone, at which point the payments cease), as opposed to a "unicorn" *defined benefit pension* (which pays the employee a predetermined amount of money, guaranteed each month of a person's retirement until they or their spouse passes, usually whichever is last).

The millennial generation has been hit with so many "once in a lifetime" financial catastrophes that it is getting hard to count them: 9/11, the dot-com bubble bursting, the housing crisis, the financial crisis, oil plummeting (hi, can you tell I live in Alberta?), the COVID-19 pandemic, and a post-pandemic recession. Seven catastrophic once-in-a-lifetime financial events and I'm only thirty-one. It seems like our generation is having some pretty bad luck, or maybe this is just how things are going to be from now on?

Becoming financially independent and amassing wealth are different now than they were thirty years ago. Policies that affect how we amass wealth could help our generation gain our financial footing. Building a society that supports wealth generation of twenty- and thirty-somethings will ensure that we aren't left behind.

I'll give you an example.

Imagine a world where wages keep up with inflation; in that world, minimum wage is $23 an hour[11] (or $50,000 a year). Although we are moving in the right direction with continued increases to minimum wage in the Western world, there is still a lot of work to be done. For example, we don't index minimum wage to inflation, meaning we don't increase minimum wage proportionally as the cost of living increases. This is odd when you consider that we increase tax brackets, TFSA (Tax-Free Savings Account) or Roth IRA (individual retirement account) contributions, and many tax deductions in step with the rate of inflation. Those tax breaks typically benefit the rich, whereas increasing minimum wage to reflect inflation would be beneficial for those with lower incomes. Our governments tend to only index specific things to inflation when it benefits the rich.

In this feminist utopia, we completely subsidize childcare, recognizing it as a basic need, and give parents flexible time off to raise the next generation. We don't have to look far to find great examples of how to support parents with young children with financially feminist policies. Quebec offers $7 per day childcare, and Sweden offers 480 days of parental leave to use before a child is eight years old. These policies allow parents the flexibility to care for their children while still working, something everyone benefits from.

Lastly, in our fictional feminist society, we close the gender wage gap by mandating disclosures that wages are fair, the way they do in Iceland, and by giving employees the legal right to know the salaries of their gender counterparts, as they do in Germany. Knowledge is power.

These are a few examples I've come across in my research—such policies are out there.[12] We can build a sustainable financial future if we mix strong, supportive policies with good money choices.

We all want to build a better life for our children, a world with less financial anxiety and dread. Many of us feel like we can't live up to the financial standards or lifestyles of our parents. But we can flip the narrative about how to build wealth.

We can build a society to set right the changes we have seen in the last thirty years, and we will find ourselves with a happier, healthier, and wealthier world.

2

TAKE BACK THE FIGHT

N THE early 1970s at the University of South Florida, a group of women marched together to "take back the night"—protesting the sexual violence against women that was happening on campus. Over the decades, the movement grew into a global phenomenon to raise awareness and empower individuals to fight sexual violence in all forms.

I encourage you, as a financial feminist, to "take back the fight"—that is, to take the power of your money into your own hands so that together we can remedy women's financial undereducation and all of the other inequities. Let's not wait 250-plus years for women's financial equality. Let's demolish that gap entirely!

We work so damn hard to earn the money that is deposited into our bank accounts, so we need to be prepared to spend some time managing it.

Women are about to gain a ton of wealth. The most poignant statistic I've encountered is that women are coming into $30 trillion[1] (yes, that's with a *T*) of wealth by the end of the decade. This epic transfer of wealth to women reflects the fact that we are becoming high income earners; in many households, we are the breadwinners. Women live longer than their men, and we are inheriting money. It's a perfect storm for amassing financial assets.

Historically, women have not had control over their finances. It wasn't until 1964 that women in the US could even have their own bank account; we have Ruth Bader Ginsburg to thank for that.[2] Given this legacy and the relatively recent gains (again, hands up for RBG), it's easy to imagine why many women, especially in cis-heterosexual relationships, still don't have a seat at the table when it comes to their household finances.

I've spoken with enough women who have been ruined financially by a partner that "knew what he was doing" to know that women *need* (and I cannot stress this enough) to be involved in financial decisions. When we aren't involved in our financial decisions, we can end up in extremely precarious situations.

Shauna was eighteen when she met her partner and twenty-six when she married him. He made a lot of money, and so she quit her job. As a married woman, she didn't plan for her financial future or save money, because she always had money that he earned. She never imagined that the man she adored and who adored her would not support her.

Fast-forward to when she was thirty-four and leaving her marriage. She found out that her husband had spent a *lot* without telling her, which meant that she walked away from the marriage with two small children and without financial resources. She continued on in denial about money; she never focused on what was happening in her bank account, hoping things would work themselves out.

Eventually though, your finances catch up to you, and Shauna was in a precarious situation with no savings or emergency fund should she face a stroke of bad financial luck. After turning forty-one, she started saving for emergencies, retirement, and for her children—not wanting to be financially reliant on a man. So often people enter marriages or long-term relationships without clear agreements on who is going to do what financially. Leaving it all to one spouse is dangerous, and women often pay the price by being left out of decisions or blindsided by the reality of their financial situation altogether.

If you don't know how much money your household has, what accounts it is in, or how it's invested, this is your wake-up call. It's time to figure it out.

The wealth women are coming into in the coming decades will translate as power. We can use this money to make positive changes—securing financial independence for ourselves, for our children, and for the benefit of all.

3

THE VALUE OF
JUDGMENT-FREE CASH

HE BURDEN of a low income brings us all down. Lifting up those who earn the least is good for our society. We have a long way to go when it comes to supporting those living at or below the poverty line. The poverty line in Canada in 2020 was $26,620 for a single person, $33,141 for two people, and $49,467 for a family of four.[1] Although taxes are relatively low at these income levels, realistically you shouldn't be paying any tax at all if you're living below the poverty line, when affording basic needs is challenging.

Sure, some might argue that there are places people can go to get some of those basics, like the food bank. But there are often barriers to accessing these places. For example, in many situations, you need to drive (which costs money) to get to a food bank. Not to mention the stigma against asking for help in a society that demands rugged individualism even while it stacks the decks against the most vulnerable.

Food banks have limitations on how frequently you can visit, and often they don't have everything you're looking for. No amount of canned goods is going to solve this problem.

I became a mom in November 2020, the height of the third wave of the COVID-19 pandemic in Alberta. Feeling overwhelmed with it all, I joined a few local Facebook groups that support new moms. Every couple of months and with increasing frequency, a mom posts (usually anonymously) that she can't afford food for her family. One mom anxiously reached out to me because the food bank didn't have baby food available for her little one. Sometimes these women don't have money for gas. I've even read of women resorting to stealing food for their child because they can't afford it.

When I read such stories, I feel despair. How are we as a society failing women so badly that they feel such shame and embarrassment, that they feel they have to anonymously plead on social media for help feeding their children?

Of course, we can individually help the people that our society is leaving in the dust. I've sent those in need cash or grocery store gift cards directly. I've also asked my online community to give to women who need resources, sometimes raising up to $1,300 per mama. That cash makes a real difference in their lives.

Our society has convinced us not to give people this one resource they actually need—cash. Although it is nice to offer to buy someone a sandwich or a coffee, it implies that we have the right to choose how women spend the money we give them, which is inherently paternalistic and demeaning. What if the thing they really need is to save up enough to purchase a form of government ID so they can open a bank account? What if they need to reload data on their phone so they can continue to apply for jobs? How would a sandwich help in this situation?

In *Give People Money*, Annie Lowrey suggests that instead of leveraging matching programs for consumer goods, such as TOMS shoes' buy-one-give-one program, we give people cash. (TOMS has since moved away from the BOGO program to a grassroots-investing model.) Studies[2] have shown that when you give people money, they spend it relatively responsibly. Not that it's any of our business what people spend their money on. (And if you really want to get pissed off about what people spend their money on, just take a look at some billionaires. You'll be really mad.) My point is, often we don't know what people need, so let them decide, judgment free, what they do with the money you are willing to give them. After all, you wouldn't like it if someone gave you money that had super-specific terms tied to it, would you? Would you want the gift-giver to tell you how to spend the cash?

Let's stop judging the lowest-income earners in our society—and instead let's lift them up.

4

PAYMENT ISN'T BIASED; THE PAYER IS

AYDAY LOANS are predatory: they have high interest rates and terrible, sneaky terms that wreak havoc on people's finances. Women are more likely than men to have to use high interest lending options, since on average they make less money than men and are more likely to work in precarious jobs. Being a single mother is one of the largest factors forcing women into poverty. When they cannot get approval for lower interest loans, payday loans are the only alternative.

Payday loans are insidious. The Criminal Code in Canada says organizations can't charge more than 60 percent on a loan, so payday lenders charge a fee each time a loan is renewed, and the terms of payday loans are typically only two weeks. That's how they skirt this rule. So, let's say the fee is $19 for every $100 borrowed, and someone borrows $1,000. That adds up to $190 to borrow $1,000, or 19 percent. That's on par with a credit card, right?

Wrong.

Because if a borrower doesn't pay back that $1,000 within the two-week term, the loan expires and she needs to renew her loan—the $190 fee will be applied again. So, if she cannot pay back the loan for a year, that adds up to twenty-six terms of two weeks each. The real cost of the $1,000 loan is $4,940—that's 394 percent interest. Highway robbery.

Payday lenders prey on vulnerable low-income people, and frankly, the practice should be illegal. ACORN Canada, an independent national organization that advocates for the rights of people with low and moderate incomes, has come out with a fantastic list of steps provinces and territories can take to change lending laws.[1]

- Mandate the banks to provide access to low interest credit for emergencies

- Mandate the banks to provide low interest overdraft protection

- Mandate the banks to provide no holds on checks

- Mandate the banks to lower NSF fees from $45 to $10

- Create a fund to support alternatives to predatory lenders

- Create a federal anti-predatory lending strategy

- Create a real time national tracking system (or database) to help stop roll over loans

- Amend the Criminal Code to lower the maximum interest rate from 60% to 30%[2]

Women are disproportionately affected by predatory lending, and we need to put a stop to the practice.

These eight policies are a great place to start when making lending more equitable for marginalized groups. Women are disproportionately affected by predatory lending, and we need to put a stop to the practice.

Organizations you can trust

So, how do you know where to go if you need money or other financial support? One trick I use to figure out if an organization or an individual has my best interest at heart is to look at how they are compensated. This shows you their bias.

For example, think of a realtor. How do they get paid?

They get paid a percentage of the price that the home is sold for. It is in their financial interest to get the most money possible, meaning they are incentivized to sell the house at a higher price. They may not be the best person to help you negotiate the lowest possible price. That doesn't mean you should avoid realtors; it just allows you to understand what they may be inclined to do. Knowing a person's biases allows you to make better decisions. You might decide that you're going to offer a lower price than what your realtor advises, and you may instruct them to push back harder than they suggest.

You can also ask similar questions about a financial institution.

How does the organization make money? Is it on the interest you pay them? Are they funded by another lending organization? Who are they owned by? Or are they a non-profit with a mandate to help citizens?

The latter is probably the best choice for your financial well-being. There are nonprofit organizations, such as Money Mentors here in Alberta, that offer credit counselling, debt consolidation, and financial education. With locations across Canada, the Credit Counselling Society is typically the safest place to look for help. Organizations like these can help you consolidate debt and negotiate payments with creditors.

5

CASHLESS

ASH ISN'T KING. Cash was on its way out before the COVID-19 pandemic hit, and the pandemic accelerated the process. This is problematic for several reasons—the first being that it creates a barrier for the unbanked to pay for things. *Unbanked* refers to people who are not served by any financial institution; they do not have a bank account, and cash is the only way they can pay for things. In Canada, 3 percent[1] of the population is unbanked—over a million people. That number increases dramatically depending on where you live: 50 percent of the population of Argentina is unbanked, and 15 percent of the population is unbanked in Greece.[2]

As a society, we need to be wary of certain practices as we move into a digital-first, or digital-only, approach to our money. The death of cash removes some people's ability to buy food and pay for basic necessities. Without solutions available for those who are unbanked, we will see increased levels of poverty.

The all-important credit score

Alex is a financially smart woman who decided she would move from Canada to San Diego for a job opportunity. She and her husband sold their home and set off on their adventure by the ocean. What they didn't realize is that they would face an impossible task of renting a home when no rental company would consider their Canadian credit score, even though they had great credit in Canada. They looked at dozens of places, but with no credit score in the US, it was extremely challenging to find a place to live.

Although this isn't a common situation, it illustrates the negative impact that not having a credit score, or having a poor credit score, can have on your life.

Your ability to obtain credit impacts your ability to leverage credit. One of the main factors in a credit score, which allows you to borrow, is credit history. As we move to a more digital world, your credit score is becoming increasingly important. Landlords may request your credit score before they approve you for a rental, and if you plan on buying a house or borrowing money, it's a good idea to make sure that your credit score is in good shape. You don't need a perfect 900 (the highest score), but you do need a credit score of about 600 to 680 if you want to buy a house,[3] per the Canadian mortgage rules that came out in 2021.

Five factors affect your credit score: [4]

1   **History of payments (35 percent).** Because this criteria makes up more than a third of your credit score, several late payments can tremendously affect your rating.

Timely payment is definitely something to focus on if you're trying to increase your credit score.

2 **Utilization (30 percent).** This is how much of your available credit you are using. If all the credit available to you is maxed out, then you are less likely to be approved for more. You typically want your used credit to be below 30 percent of the total available to you.

3 **Length of credit history (15 percent).** The longer an account has been open, the better it is for your credit score. Keep your longest-running credit card open.

4 **Different types of credit (10 percent).** Having different types of financial products increases your credit score. Think mortgages, student loans, lines of credit, and credit cards all as different products.

5 **Inquiries on your credit (10 percent).** The number of new products you apply for impacts your credit score, especially if you have several credit checks in a short period of time.

If you can do it, pay off your credit card *in full every month*. If you can't do that, make sure you pay more than the minimum payment, so that you are reducing the balance and not only paying off the interest. That being said, don't charge something to your credit card and then immediately pay it off if you're trying to build your credit score. The credit bureau (the company that dictates your score) may not register any activity on the card: when they check your cards once a month, they need to see that there was a balance owing and that you subsequently paid it off within the twenty-one-day grace period before you are charged interest.

Women on average have lower credit scores than men, which could be for a number of factors. I'd suggest that it's because we are approved for less credit, which leads to higher use of fewer sources of credit. Also, in many cases a woman is the secondary card holder on her husband's card and therefore does not build her own credit score.

One of my favorite Canadian fintech (financial technology) companies, Borrowell, is a great option to check your credit score and monitor it for free; Borrowell can also suggest how to improve your credit score (#NotSponsored).

If you're struggling to build your credit or you have trouble managing your credit cards, try using technology to your advantage. Companies like KOHO and Stack offer prepaid Mastercards that help you manage and track your spending. This technology allows you to transfer money from your bank to the card, which you then use like a credit card. They also offer products such as monthly microloans to help you build your credit slowly.

6

SMASH
STUDENT DEBT

MY POSTSECONDARY education has afforded me a lot of opportunity in life and is one of the main reasons I can live the lifestyle I do. My degree has allowed me to pursue a well-respected designation and earn six figures; it's unlikely I would have been able to do so without a university education. My parents paid for my university tuition, and it's one of the best gifts they have given me. I didn't have student loan payments eating into my ability to pay rent or put food on the table. I started saving and investing earlier than my peers, taking advantage of matching programs my employer offered when I was starting out. Everyone should have this advantage, but not everyone's parents have the means to pay their tuition.

Student loans are a sham, and the cost of postsecondary education is an even bigger sham. Well-educated people make for a stronger and more self-reliant society, lifting all of us into a better position and ultimately costing our society less.[1] Charging students tens or even hundreds of thousands of dollars for a degree sounds like robbery to me, and charging interest on those loans is even worse.

The average student debtor graduates with $28,000 debt here in Canada[2] and $40,904 in the US.[3] This balloons by approximately $15,000 to $20,000 when you include student lines of credit, personal loans, and credit card debt.[4] When you compare this to the average starting salary of $54,000, it's no wonder our new grads are poor. Women hold 58 percent of all student debt and have on average 9.6 percent[5] more debt just one year after graduation than men do. The statistics are more abysmal when we look at marginalized groups: for example, LGBTQ2S+ individuals on average have $16,000 more in student loan debt[6] than cis-heterosexual people do.

Most student loans here in Canada are to be repaid within ten years. So if you owe $50,000 on a government loan, you're required to pay $5,000 a year, or $416 a month, for ten years. If you earn the average salary of $54,000, your after-tax income could be anywhere from $3,500 to $3,700 per month, depending on the province you live in. That makes your required debt payment more than 10 percent of your take-home pay.

If these numbers feel overwhelming to you, you're not alone in feeling that way—and there may be options for you.

In Canada, the Repayment Assistance Plan (RAP) can help you with cash flow. As of November 2022, the RAP eligibility has a zero-payment income threshold and maximum payments have been lowered from 20 to 10 percent of household income.[7] In addition, interest accumulation has

Charging students tens or even hundreds of thousands of dollars for a degree sounds like robbery, and charging interest on those loans is even worse.

been permanently eliminated going forward. After ten years of RAP, the government covers the principal and interest that exceeds your reduced monthly payments, and what you owe will decrease, with your loan gradually being paid off.

Although interest paid on student loans is deductible on tax returns, it's important that we continue to push the government to make postsecondary education more affordable and accessible. This can be done by eradicating student loan debt, with proposals such as the one put forward by Canada's New Democratic Party for $20,000 of loan forgiveness. In the US, President Joe Biden's student loan forgiveness program cancels a portion of student debt for forty million student loan borrowers.[8]

Whatever you do, I encourage you to stay in good standing when it comes to your payments. In Canada, student loans are not written off if you file for bankruptcy within seven years of finishing your studies, and if you miss nine months of payments, your student loan will be sent to collections. If you're overwhelmed by your payments, contact the National Student Loans Service Centre to work out a payment plan.

7

OUT-WAGED

WE HEAR the term *wage gap* thrown around a lot. What is the wage gap? Does it exist? Is it all just made up?

As mentioned earlier in the book, the wage gap sits at around 83 cents on the dollar—this means that women on average earn 16 cents less per dollar than men do for the exact same work. Now I'm sure that someone is going to tell me that paying people differently for the same work is illegal, and that's true. But the wage gap is so much larger than just paying two people differently for the same role. And when you factor in race, sexuality, and/or class, the wage gap grows.

There is a lot to unpack, so buckle up.

The systems we have set up in the world of work disproportionately hurt women. To start, women are twice as likely to be in part-time jobs. Part-time roles typically pay less per hour than full-time roles, and part-time workers miss out on advantages such as health benefits or retirement contributions, which full-time positions often offer.

The burden of care for children and the elderly often falls to women. On average, women spend less time at the office, even if they work full-time, making them less likely to be tapped for networking events and travel opportunities compared to their male counterparts who don't have to leave early to pick up the kids from school. We all know how many impromptu conversations about career opportunities take place at drinks after work or on the golf course. If you're dashing off to pick up the kids and logging in to your laptop from home, then you are likely missing out on these discussions that translate into promotions and raises. When managers are looking at who to promote, they are subconsciously biased toward the employees they spend the most time with or see in the office the most.[1]

Women are also passed over for promotions because of how they are mentored and what managers use to measure performance. Men and women tend to be mentored very differently. In her TED Talk "The Career Advice You Probably Didn't Get," Susan Colantuono says that managers of any gender often mentor women for their soft skills[2] and men for their analytical or technical skills, which often convert into solid and specific metrics a manager can use when deciding on a promotion. Women more often than not also find themselves taking on "non-promotable tasks," like organizing social events for the office. In addition, men are often promoted based on what they promise they can do in a role, whereas women are judged based on their past accomplishments.

On the one hand, women apply less frequently for jobs for which they aren't 100 percent qualified. Men, on the other hand, apply for a job when they meet 40 to 60 percent of the qualifications.[3] Lastly, there are biases in hiring practices. A study was done on two groups of people analyzing two résumés.[4] Everything about the résumés was identical other than the name at the top. In one group, the candidate had a masculine name, John, and in the other, a feminine name, Jennifer. The results of this comparison of fictitious résumés were that the group with John's résumé were much more likely to hire him, and they offered him a starting salary about $13,000 higher than those with Jennifer. The biases in our hiring practices and how we view the competencies of women are deeply flawed at a systemic level, and it will take years of unlearning to untangle these knots.

If you don't think a gender pay gap exists, I encourage you to look within your organization and ask. I did. Turns out, I was training a man for the same role I was in, and he was earning $13,000 more than I was. At the time, I was earning $57,000, so $13,000 was a 23 percent pay difference.

When I found this out, my first instinct was to feel shame and embarrassment. Why had I not looked into this earlier? Why hadn't I negotiated harder? Was I not worth as much as he was?

It didn't seem right to be paid this little for the *exact same role*.

Women make up 50 percent of the world's population and comprise around 50 percent of the workforce—we should be paid the same as men.

When women are paid less than men, they unsurprisingly end up with less disposable income. This means they

All people should be paid equally, regardless of gender.

have less money to save and to invest. The wage gap turns into a savings and investing gap, fueling the wealth gap (which we'll talk about more in the next chapter). Globally, women only hold 30 percent[5] of all wealth. Our holdings are going up, but we aren't where we need to be yet.

Getting passed over for a promotion means you're paid less even if you have the same experience or same accomplishments as a male counterpart. A lower starting salary becomes a lower subsequent raise for each pay increase and promotion that follows, resulting in lower lifetime earnings.

When considering the wage gap, many people only want to compare two individuals in the same role to see if there is a gap. Doing so does usually show a gap of about 3 percent, which over the span of a career can mean hundreds of thousands of dollars. But the gap is much more insidious than this. There are also fewer women in upper management and C-suite positions and fewer women in higher paying industries (like tech); women are more likely to be in part-time jobs; and women are promoted at slower rates than men.

It's not an apples to apples comparison; it's more apples to oranges—and all of the great benefits and flexible work arrangements are given to the oranges. The following graph illustrates this well, with women represented by apples. You can see how this crispy fall fruit is concentrated in entry level positions that have lower earnings. The men are illustrated by the oranges, and these citrus wonders are concentrated in higher paying fields with larger earning potential. Even when we get to the highest paying C-suite positions, there is still a wage gap: men in C-suite positions are often paid more and/or are in larger organizations.

A System at Work

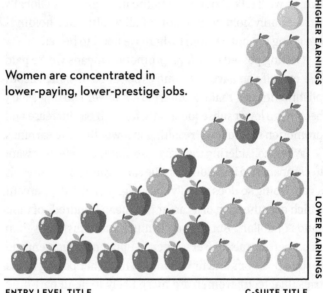

Women are concentrated in
lower-paying, lower-prestige jobs.

HIGHER EARNINGS

LOWER EARNINGS

ENTRY LEVEL TITLE   C-SUITE TITLE

Some people argue that women choose lower income,
entry level, or part-time work so they can have more flexibility. But that is inaccurate. In many career paths, lower
wages follow high participation of women in a specific field.
Women were the original computer engineers and they
were underpaid and undervalued.[6] As time went on, the
field employed more men, and today we see an extremely
high concentration of men in this field, demanding hand-
some salaries. Tech is one of the highest paid industries.

Teaching is an example that goes the other way. Originally this profession was dominated by men; over time, it became women-dominated, and there is a lack in prestige and pay associated with that. Pediatrics is starting to follow suit with 64 percent[7] of doctors in this specialty being women; it has become the lowest paid medical specialty.[8] These factors continue to pile on and create a complex and nuanced sexist system in which men earn much more than women.

8

PERPETUATING
THE GAP

W E'VE TALKED about the wage gap. Now it's time
to understand how that becomes the wealth gap.
The wage gap is alive and well, and as a result of
it, women have less income to save and ultimately
invest, meaning they accumulate less wealth than men over
a lifetime.

The wealth gap has grown exponentially over the last
thirty to forty years. The world's richest 1 percent have twice
as much wealth as the other 6.9 billion people combined.[1]
If that's not inequality, I don't know what is. In 1965, the
average CEO's salary compared to the average salary of an
employee at the same company was 20 to 1, meaning CEOs
made twenty times more money than their employees.
Fast-forward to 2018 and the ratio was a staggering 278 to 1.[2]
When we look at the top Fortune 500 companies, 92 percent
of the CEOs are men.[3] In the last decade, we have seen
average wages increase by only about 3 percent, while the

average dividend to shareholders has increased by 31 percent. We are transferring wealth from the working class to the elite.

What do I mean by the *elite*? The top 0.01 percent who make hundreds of millions of dollars a year, amassing billions in wealth.[4]

If you're not convinced there's a wealth gap between men and women, know that men have 50 percent more wealth than women do worldwide, and that the twenty-two richest men in the world own more wealth than all of the women in Africa.[5] Does that seem fair to you?

Billionaires should probably be illegal.

Mikel Jollett tweeted, "OK how about this: No more billionaires. None. After you reach $999 million, every red cent goes to schools and health care. You get a trophy that says, 'I won capitalism' and we name a dog park after you."[6]

Absolutely. Perfect.

I don't think many people understand just how much a billion dollars is. We understand a million, sure, but try wrapping your mind around how much a billion is.

Look at it this way: if you had saved $10,000 per day since the building of the pyramids, you would still only have a fifth of the average wealth of the five richest billionaires. Read that again. Four thousand years of saving $10,000 a day, and you still aren't even at the top. Billionaires do not *earn* their money—they accumulate it thanks to the wild profits our broken capitalistic society creates for them. There is no reason Jeff Bezos should make $200,000 per minute[7] (while the average person makes 10 cents), or that the billionaires of the US increased their wealth by $637 billion[8] during the pandemic while the average American received a total of $600 in pandemic support. Billionaires aren't working two million times harder than the rest of us, so why are they being compensated as if they are?

Billionaires support the massive, continued transfer of wealth from the working and middle classes to the richest 1 percent.

Right up there with billionaires' accumulation of capital is the travesty of unpaid caregiving work that compounds the wealth gap. Globally, women and girls put in 12.5 billion hours per day of unpaid care work. We would add $12 trillion to the global economy per year if we began paying women and girls minimum wage for their unpaid caregiving work. Additionally, 42 percent of women can't get jobs because they are caregivers.[9] Meanwhile, the household work that as recently as fifty years ago was commonly performed by men has been mostly outsourced. Men used to do things like fix the car and be handy around the house, maybe do some plumbing; nowadays most people typically call on tradespeople to do these jobs, but the same is not true for women's work. Women are by and large still responsible for keeping the house clean, cooking, and caring for the elderly and the young.

PART

2

Build Wealth for Self-Care

"They'll tell you you're too loud—that you need to wait your turn and ask the right people for permission. Do it anyway."

ALEXANDRIA OCASIO-CORTEZ

S ELF-CARE IS defined as "the practice of taking action to preserve or improve one's own health."[1] People do many different things to practice self-care: work out, meditate, maybe even have a glass of wine in a bubble bath.

I'm here to tell you that building your wealth is a form of self-care.

Money is stressful; we're usually worried that there isn't going to be enough of it. Building wealth means having a financial cushion to rely on if life takes a turn for the worse.

At the beginning of the pandemic, for example, many people that thought they were going to lose their jobs. Around the globe, people were being laid off—and fast. We weren't ready. Half of Americans and one-third of Canadians[2] don't have three months of savings, and one-quarter have no emergency fund at all.[3]

The chapters in this part offer strategies for you to develop financial self-care, beginning with your mindset and extending into practical tactics so that you are building wealth to ease your money-related stress and take financial feminism into your own hands.

9

FINANCIAL FEELINGS

ANY FINANCIAL experts will tell you to "take the emotion out of investing" or "stop the impulse purchase," and you'll be on your way to a cushy retirement. But let's get real. Money is very personal and very emotional.

Our money stories are shaped from a very young age. The anecdote I shared earlier about my very first small business venture (the lemonade stand) was a memory from early childhood. We usually don't realize the impact of these money stories and the lessons we learned (subconsciously or consciously) from our parents on our daily relationship with money.

If you were taught that there was never enough money to make ends meet, you may hold the belief that there will never be enough money and you need to hoard it. Take Jenn, a good friend of mine. Money was always tight in her household: there were times when her family would go to the grocery store and pick the cheapest things off the shelf for dinner. At the checkout, her mom would casually throw in a $5 magazine. What message did that send her children, who had just watched her fret over which brand of pasta to buy? (Spoiler alert: the no-name brand always won.)

These personal money stories shape how we spend money and approach our finances as adults. Often, they are deeply rooted in shame, and the narrative tells us we aren't worthy of having or spending our money in ways that we enjoy. Psychology plays a huge role in our behaviors toward money, though the financial system seems to deny this personal aspect of money. We also tend to ignore any trauma around money that we may have experienced growing up, as well as the impact of colonization on our finances. Those who have the most control over money in society tend to talk about and deal with it as though money is as logical as math. But the heart of capitalism depends on the emotions that propel us to buy more. Just think of the stereotypical middle-aged man and his shiny new sports car, the impulse purchases after a breakup, the lineups for the latest version of the iPhone. Our financial system is set up to feed on our emotions.

You are *not* bad with money

When I speak to women about money, they often say they aren't math people, aren't good at numbers, or are bad with money. They have been told from a young age that women fit into these stereotypes, so they feel overwhelmed with their financial situation and have no idea where to start. Women still get the message today that they need to find a

Personal money stories shape how **we approach our finances as adults.**

husband who can provide for them, so they won't have to worry about a thing financially.[1]

The reality is that women tend to have traits and habits that are aligned with good money management skills: we are risk aware, we are less likely to move investments around during market fluctuations (and therefore our investments perform better over the long term), and we tend to save sooner than men.[2]

Owning your financial narrative and ultimately your financial future is empowering, and it will lower your financial stress. Although it can be overwhelming to get started, I want you to remind yourself repeatedly that *you are not bad with money*. You are learning. Wherever you are in your money journey, chances are you don't know it all. That's okay. Approach your financial education as a journey and with a beginner's mindset. Consume information, bolster your financial knowledge, and make the best decisions you can with the information you have.

What do you value?

Values play a huge role in how you manage your money. James W. Frick reportedly quipped, "Don't tell me where your priorities are. Show me where you spend your money and I'll tell you what they are."[3]

Starting with your values is such an important way to approach your finances. If you don't value what you spend your money on, you will feel broke and deprived. Take me, for example. If I purchase my lunch whenever I go into the office, I'm not adding a lot of value to my life. Food court meals are mediocre at best and probably cost me $15 to $20. To paraphrase Marie Kondo, this food doesn't spark joy in my life, and I can think of a zillion more value-add ways that I'd rather spend $100 a week, or $400 a month.

Outlining your values will help you clarify how to spend your money. So let's get clear. What are the top three things you value? I'll give you an example of what this looks like for me. My top three values are:

1 Spending time with the people I love and care about most (my baby and my hubby).

2 Exploring the world.

3 Feeling financially secure.

Back to my lunch example. If instead of going to the food court, I pack my own lunch, I can take that $400 a month and spend it on a nice dinner date with my husband (and on a babysitter), and I can feel guilt-free about dropping cash on a nice bottle of wine at dinner. I might even have money left over from that $400 to put toward a future trip.

Knowing what's important to you helps you define where to allocate your money, which is a basic premise of budgeting. I don't *love* the b-word, because for many people budgeting feels restrictive. And restriction of any diet, whether it's financial or caloric, leads to bingeing. A better way to look at budgeting is as the best allocation of the fixed resources (your money) available to you. Think of it as a spending plan for your hard-earned dollars.

Take some time to sift through where you spend the most money each month. Look at a couple of months' worth of your spending to spot patterns, and list your top three to five categories (for example, meals out, clothes, groceries, events). Then you can compare these spending categories to your values. Is your spending in line with your values? Are you spending a lot on skincare and massages—and you're good with it because you love pampering yourself and you do it with friends, and you adore this social time together? Great! But if you're spending a lot on a beauty regimen and it's not in line with your values—you might want to rethink it. Do your purchases spark joy? How much happiness do you get from your current spending? Is this purchase going to add to your happiness?

Money is a tool, and you have the power to pick and choose how you allocate it. Ensuring that your spending is in line with your values is the first step. Becoming aware of spending patterns that don't add value to your life allows you to take a critical look at the changes you want to make in your spending habits.

Personal finance is just that: personal. There is no right or wrong way to spend your money. But we love to judge people, usually women, on their purchases. In the personal finance space, you may hear things like "Spending on luxury goods is a waste" or "You should always buy the cheapest used car because they depreciate in value." But the truth is, what adds value to your life is likely different from what adds value for the person next to you. It doesn't matter what you spend your money on, as long as it makes you happy and you aren't racking up debt. Hell, if you want to collect stamps with all your extra cash, by all means. Some people may think spending a few hundred dollars on a dinner out is a grotesque waste of money, but it's something I enjoy doing with my husband and it makes our relationship stronger. Worth it.

I'm giving you permission to spend your money on what makes sense and is in line with your values. If that's a $3,000 Louis Vuitton bag, go for it (provided the cost is not going to sit on a credit card and accrue interest). If you can afford it and it will add to your happiness, why not? Maybe that $3,000 bag allows you to feel like you've made it. Indulge.

10

LATTES AND LIES

IMPULSE SPENDING can be detrimental to building your financial empire as well as detrimental to how women are perceived in society.

How often have you overheard (or been part of) a conversation between women about how much they just spent on an unplanned trip to the mall? Lord knows there are enough movies and TV shows out there that characterize women as ditzy spendthrifts who can't seem to help themselves when they see a sale. (*Confessions of a Shopaholic*, I'm looking at you.) It's as though we as women are *expected* to behave this way, as if overspending comes with being a woman. A 2018 Starling Bank study of magazine articles about money[1] found that content geared toward men was mainly focused on investing, while material aimed at women told them to spend less. Our media has biases about how women and men manage and spend their money. It's coming at us from all sides.

The forty-eight-hour rule

Over a decade ago, I was trying to rein in my spending. I had gone through a bad breakup and was spending money on anything and everything. Manicures, check. New hair, check. Massage, check. Starbucks, new outfits, dining out: check, check, check.

Impulse spending is purely emotional: every swipe of the credit or debit card releases dopamine, the happy hormone inside our brain. It's addictive, especially for someone who lacks dopamine naturally, like myself. Only when you tackle this head-on will you be able to get out of the vicious cycle.

In *Confessions of a Shopaholic*, the main character, Rebecca, maxes out twelve credit cards to avoid dealing with her emotions and everything going on in her life. This fictional story plays into a stereotype: women are taught to manage negative experiences by shopping. Frankly, it's unhealthy both emotionally and financially. At $200 an hour, therapy would have been a cheaper option for me (and probably Rebecca) and definitely more effective.

I knew my spending wasn't sustainable. Coming to terms with that fact meant setting some parameters for what I was allowed to spend money on.

Enter the forty-eight-hour rule.

It's pretty simple actually, and there are many versions of it floating around the personal finance sphere. Marketers and salespeople are damn good at what they do; they know how to lure you into making a purchase early and often. Have you ever said you were going to think about a purchase and had a salesperson tell you they're not sure if there would be any of the product left by the time you decided? Scarcity tactics are a great way to close a sale, and commission-based employees know that. When I worked in retail, we were *trained* to use that tactic. The more sales we closed, the higher up on the leaderboard we were. The hamster wheel of capitalism continues.

The forty-eight-hour rule dictates that before you make an impulse purchase (something you didn't plan and save for), you must give yourself at least forty-eight hours to figure out if you actually want it. Buyer's remorse is a powerful negative emotion and you want to avoid it.

By giving yourself forty-eight hours, you'll be able to see if:

1 You can afford it.
2 You still want it.
3 The price is better somewhere else.

Nine times out of ten, I've found that by leaving the store or closing the website, I completely forget about the item I *had to have* only moments before. Following this rule will help you financially manage those impulse purchases that can add up in a hurry.

Sorry, David Bach

When I first entered the personal finance space, I read *The Automatic Millionaire* by David Bach, and it truly piqued my interest. It led me to start saving, investing, and managing my spending the way I do. I owe a lot to David Bach, but in

The latte
factor **is a lie.**

my twelve-plus years as a personal finance expert, I can tell you that ordering a latte (or avocado toast) won't make or break your finances (as Bach suggests it might).

Here's the truth: the latte factor is a lie. Its whole premise is that if you save money rather than make small daily purchases, on things like lattes, and you invest it, over the long haul you'll grow your wealth.

Basically, if you give up lattes, you'll be a millionaire.

People may have rightly followed this advice a decade ago, but so much has changed in the last ten years that this approach is now irrelevant. For twenty- and thirty-somethings, skyrocketing costs of postsecondary education, an overinflated housing market, and wage stagnation are the true culprits of our inability to get ahead financially. We are worse off than our parents' generation, and women are hit twice as hard with the wage gap.

Although ditching the coffee habit may seem like a smart financial decision, you may end up feeling deprived in the long run and give up any savings or investing goals. You are in control of how you spend your money, but there are larger macroeconomic factors at play that influence you more than you may know.

The crux of the latte argument is that if you give up small pleasures that you pay for on a frequent basis, you will become a millionaire.[2] But $5 a day over three years, say, is not going to be enough to get you there. A $5 latte bought five days a week equals $1,300 a year—not enough to do anything substantial with.

Don't overpay for large items

As we already talked about, there is something to be said for cutting spending on things you don't value, but in my humble opinion, if you're looking at the small stuff, like lattes, you're looking in the wrong place.

Focus your attention on the bigger ticket items. For example, if you can cut your insurance or rent by a few hundred dollars a month, that will add up a lot faster than $20 per week on lattes. Negotiating thousands off a car, or even tens of thousands off a home, not only means you'll pay less back to the bank for the loan over the long term, but you'll also decrease the amount of interest you pay. Going after savings on the high value big-ticket items gives you the ability to save thousands; it's a much smarter financial focus than cutting out something you enjoy indulging in. It's not always an option, but this can be a great option to get ahead financially.

11

THE PAIN OF PAYMENT

THE PAIN of payment goes hand in hand with the concept of mental accounting, which was introduced to me a few years back by personal finance author Preet Banerjee. According to The Decision Lab, "Mental accounting explains how we tend to assign subjective value to our money, usually in ways that violate basic economic principles. Although money has consistent, objective value, the way we go about spending it is often subject to different rules, depending on how we earned the money, how we intend to use it, and how it makes us feel."[1]

Mental accounting means we treat money differently, depending on what it's earmarked for or how we received the cash in the first place. If you were to come into a windfall, you might purchase a luxury good. Conversely, we might never buy that luxury good if it meant spending money from our paycheck—even though the dollars hold the same value.

Think back to when you were a teen. If you were like me, you may have spent some of your downtime at the mall shopping with friends. At fourteen years old, I would walk through West Edmonton Mall with my Guess purse in hand and a few hundred dollars in my wallet. Cold hard cash was how I saved and spent all my money back then. Purchasing a sweater at Hollister or Abercrombie & Fitch meant handing over four crisp twenties to the cashier. Parting with that cash was inherently painful; it felt like I was parting with a limb.

Fast-forward a couple of years and I was spending predominantly with my debit card. Debit card purchases were not nearly as painful as giving up cash, but the effects were still in real time. The money left my bank account as soon as I completed the purchase. But it was easier to part with more money than I'd intended to spend.

Credit cards are a breeze to swipe or tap, and you don't see the damage of your spending until twenty-one days after the purchase—which can make them inherently troublesome. I'm sure most of us can recall a time when we opened our credit card statement and thought, *I spent HOW MUCH?! That can't be right!* But it usually is.

Think about how technology enables us to have a less stressful, more pain-free experience. You likely have an option to pay for things by tapping your phone at the point of sale. How many times do you reach for your phone in a day? I can tell you. On average in the US, a person reaches for their phone 344 times per day.[2] It's an ingrained habit. We don't even think about it.

The shift to digital will only exacerbate the problem of pain-free spending—that is, disassociating from the impact of spending means we will find ourselves with more debt and more unhappiness than ever before.

So what are we supposed to do?

Becoming aware of how easy it is to fall into the impulse spending trap is the first step. If you know the tactics that the marketers use against you (Sephora, I see you in my inbox), then you can address the problem head-on. Changing how you manage your money can be another good approach. Reducing your use of traditional credit cards and Apple Pay may make it easier to rein in impulse spending.

You can use an app to track your spending, such as Mint or YNAB (You Need A Budget). (KOHO is another option for Canadians.) With prepaid credit cards like KOHO's, you can load cash from your paycheck onto the card and spend from there, and you can use this credit card to pay digitally.

A benefit of the KOHO app in particular is that it will alert you of your new spendable balance after each purchase. If you load $100 onto the card and buy something for $20, the app automatically notifies you that you only have $80 left to spend. This connects you to your spending and makes it a little bit more painful. It might make you think twice before swiping.

KOHO also allows you set up savings goals and gives you round-ups for your spending, and there is an integration with Wealthsimple to help you start investing as well. Say you make a purchase of $1.50: the financial company will "round it up" to $2.00 and automatically save or invest that extra 50 cents. This is a great way to get started saving and investing and is relatively painless. It also gives you a monthly summary of how, what, and when you spent all your hard-earned cash. It's one of the better apps I've seen from a financial health and wellness perspective, plus you can earn cash back using the app. It's free to use, which is wonderful, and there is a paid version that allows you to earn a higher cash-back percentage. This is a great option for individuals trying to build their credit and manage their discretionary spending.

12

PATRIARCHY-PROOF FINANCES

I OFTEN WONDER if we lull ourselves into a false sense of security by keeping too much cash on hand. For some people, this might mean physical cash in their house, but a lot of us let our checking account balance grow to a few thousand dollars just to keep our mind at ease. A former coworker once told me he kept close to $20,000 in his checking account, and I'm pretty sure I spat out my coffee when I heard that. In his mind, he was prepared should anything go wrong, but in reality, he was hampering his ability to build wealth.

Growing our wealth is one of the best ways we can fight the patriarchy. When women have more money, they have more opportunity to influence society—so we need more women with more money. Women, in general, tend to keep more money in cash than men do, with 70 percent[1] of their portfolio in cash. But money sitting in cash earns very little to no interest. With inflation in Canada hitting record highs of 7.7 percent in May 2022,[2] money earning little or nothing results in a loss of purchasing power (how much you can afford with one dollar today versus how much you'll be able to afford with that same dollar tomorrow). Any dollar growing by less than the rate of inflation is losing the power to buy things, ultimately making you, the owner of that dollar, worse off.

I'm not trying to induce unnecessary stress, but there is value in setting a maximum amount of cash to leave sitting in your checking account. You should establish that amount and put the rest of your money to work—earning a few percent in a savings account, paying down debt, or investing in your future. This is on top of a regularly funded emergency fund (which we will talk about later).

Beware of accounts with minimum balances. These types of accounts require you to keep thousands of dollars in them before fees are waived. Your money is likely sitting there losing purchasing power just to avoid a fee. And while it sits there, your bank makes a return on your cash, because banks use your deposits to invest for themselves. In fact, the bank can get a twelve-fold return on every dollar you deposit. How? They relend your money, earning interest from the next borrower, and they access high-yield, low-risk investments, like corporate bonds that have high minimums (think $100,000) and high returns. If you've ever looked at what some of the banks make in profit, your stomach probably churned. For example, TD Bank made $42 million in revenue in 2021 and $17 million in profit.[3] The best thing you can do is to find a financial institution that doesn't charge fees. There are even some (like

Tangerine and EQ Bank in Canada; Capital One and Ally in the US) that pay you interest to keep money in your checking account. Yes, please.

If you're wondering how much cash you should keep in your checking account, try this: monitor the dollar amount at which you start to feel spendy. If you can keep your checking account balance below that, you'll likely manage impulse spending better, and you may even skip that extra department store purchase. There should be enough in the account to cover one month of your expenses plus a few hundred dollars of buffer, but anything above that should be transferred to a different account, even if it's a savings account with the same bank.

More on banks

In Canada, most financial institutions are covered by the Canada Deposit Insurance Corporation (CDIC), a Crown corporation that insures against the loss of deposits in case of failure of member institutions. You want to make sure that your bank is on the CDIC's list. A lot of people seem to think that only the big banks are covered, which isn't the case. In the US, the Federal Deposit Insurance Corporation (FDIC) covers banks, and the National Credit Union Administration (NCUA) covers credit unions.

Especially when interest rates are low, it's important to stash your cash where you will get the best rate of return. Many people worry that their money is unprotected in an online bank, such as Tangerine or EQ Bank, which typically

Growing our wealth is one of the best ways we can fight the patriarchy.

offers lower fees and higher interest rates, but it is indeed protected. These online banks store your money in the same way a traditional bank does. Our currency and our banking system is digital, and when you get paid, it's just a digital increase in your account.

If your financial institution is CDIC insured, up to $100,000 in each eligible category is protected, should the bank fail (which isn't something that happens very often). Make sure the financial institution you use is covered by the regulatory body in its jurisdiction (whether that be the CDIC or otherwise). Shop around to find the best savings rate; companies like Ratehub are great for comparing rates. Look at your country's prime rate and ensure you are earning at least that amount on your savings and investments. You can also compare the rate of inflation to your savings rate. If inflation is close to 8 percent, then earning 2 percent interest in an account isn't great. You're losing 6 percent of your purchasing power.

Should you kill high interest debt first?

There are many different schools of thought about debt repayment.

Dave Ramsey says, "If you're working on paying off debt, the only time you should see the inside of a restaurant is if you're working there."[4]

Suze Orman says, "You will never, ever, ever have financial freedom if you have debt."[5]

And I'm here to tell you that it really doesn't matter what any of those experts say, because dealing with debt is a highly individualized pursuit. Paying your high interest debt first makes sense if you only consider the math—because you'll pay less in interest—but there is often an emotional component of debt repayment to consider too.

If you rack up debt because of a bad breakup or sudden loss, it may feel like an incredible emotional burden. Likewise, if you owe money to someone you know (a friend or family member), it can put a lot of strain on the relationship. Paying down that debt first, even if it is interest free, may be best for your well-being. And if you find yourself in an emotionally or financially abusive relationship with someone who holds the money you owe them over your head, pay this debt back first, as fast as you can—no matter how low the interest is—and get out of that relationship. Money can be an excellent tool, but it can also be used to control others. And that's no way for a financial feminist to live.

Financial decision fatigue

Each day women are faced with up to 35,000 decisions[6]— yes, you read that number correctly—ranging from what sweater to wear to what to have for lunch to who to hire for an open role, and everything in between. Decision fatigue is when you become overwhelmed by the number of decisions you must make in a day. If your tank is empty and you don't have the capacity to deal with your finances, why would you add money decisions to an already long and overwhelming list? A full 22 percent of women ignore their financial stress.[7] But as you now know, ignoring your money is a Pink Tax you can't afford!

One simple solution to minimize financial decision fatigue is to automate as much of your finances as you can—take bill payments and money transfers off your to-do list entirely. Make it so that you only need to quickly check in with your money each month. Don't spend time in the weeds moving money from one account to another. If you enjoy money management, your time is better spent learning to analyze and project the future power of your dollars rather than doing something that can be easily automated.

Years ago, my husband and I automated our banking transactions, and it changed the way we manage our money. Instead of worrying if we've missed a bill payment or if we remembered to move money to our savings account, we know it's all taken care of. As new parents, we are so grateful we did this, because OMG why is being a parent so exhausting and all encompassing? Because we are paid on the fifteenth and thirtieth of each month, we set up our money transfers—from checking to savings, checking to investing accounts, and checking to bills—for the sixteenth and the first. For large bills (hello, property taxes), we divide the cost over twenty-four automatic transfers and move that money into its own savings account so when we need to pay, the money's there. If your income fluctuates and you are worried about cash flow some months, you can always change the amount or defer a transfer.

The bottom line is that you have enough on your mind. Take your basic financial transactions off the constant list and lighten your mental load.

Track your progress

Tracking your progress sounds simple, but it makes such a big difference when you're looking at your psyche as it relates to finances. It's easy to be hard on yourself about money:

- I spent too much this month.
- I didn't save enough.
- I shouldn't have purchased that.

I'm sure you've said one if not all of these things to yourself before. I know I have.

But you have a choice: you can focus on the little things and beat yourself up over them. You cannot see the forest for the trees. Or you can take a step back, look at the big picture, and notice how far you've come.

The latter option is exactly what tracking your progress is about. You don't have to do it often, but even a couple of times a year will give you a good baseline for your progress. Start by calculating your net worth, which is the sum of your assets (what you own) minus your liabilities (what you owe). Take a look at the example that follows. Check in at intervals to see that it's moving in the right direction.

If your net worth is negative, don't worry too much about it—the fact is, women are more likely than men to have a lower and more negative net worth.[8] Focus on your progress. As you check in over the months and years, you want your net worth to increase. That's the direction you are heading in—but sometimes you may have less than you did the previous time you checked in. The housing or stock market may drop, or you may need to make a large

Sample Net Worth Statement

ASSETS	AMOUNT
Home	$550,000
Vehicle	$30,000
Cash (checking account)	$6,000
Savings account	$22,000
Investment accounts (TFSA, RRSP, 401K, Roth IRA)	$65,000
Children's education accounts	$30,000
Fine art	$10,000
Total assets (A)	**$713,000**

LIABILITIES	AMOUNT
Student loan	$20,000
Mortgage	$350,000
Personal loan	$2,000
Credit card debt	$500
Total liabilities (B)	**$372,500**

NET WORTH (assets minus liabilities, or A - B):	**$340,500**

purchase or repair. That's okay. Focus on the overall direction of your wealth.

I started tracking our net worth in 2012. I do it every month because that's just who I am; I do love a good Excel spreadsheet. I have ten-plus years of data, and I've watched our net worth go from $17,000 to $650,000—a 3,700 percent increase. I share these numbers not to brag but to inspire you to start amassing wealth. There were months, sometimes even years, when unexpected financial turmoil hit—job loss, study leave, unexpected expenses, maternity leave, which you can see it on the chart below—but the general trend was always up. Yours can be too. You'll also notice that more of our wealth accumulated later on in our financial journey; this is the power of compound interest.

Our Net Worth, 2012-2022

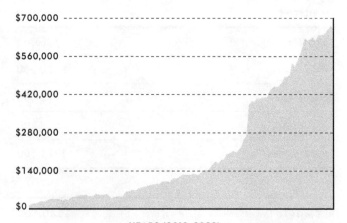

YEARS (2012-2022)

13

TAKE BACK THE BANK

S O MANY statistics out there suggest that women have poor financial literacy skills, but the truth is that the financial industry has ignored women for a long time. *Maybe* women aren't as financially literate as men, but I would argue that women haven't had the same opportunities to learn and be involved with their money decisions.

If you think back to your childhood, you can start to unpack why this might be the case. Little girls are encouraged to be quiet, caring, and cooperative. Little boys are applauded for being courageous, brave, and bold. This puts girls and young women at a disadvantage. Little girls are taught not to question authority, which could make them less likely as adults to negotiate or push financial advisers to be clear when they use financial jargon.

Boys are more likely to be streamed into the sciences and math, while girls historically have not been encouraged to pursue STEM (science, technology, engineering, and math). As evidence, take the fact that I was one of three women in my first-year engineering class. These biases lead the women of tomorrow to shy away from their finances. Although I'm generalizing here, I have heard countless women say "I'm not good at math" to excuse why they are not involved in their finances.

Here's a stone-cold fact: you don't need to be good at math to manage your finances. So what if you can't solve equations in your head? You probably have a calculator on you at all times on your phone, and contrary to what your teachers told you, there's nothing wrong with using it.

You are capable of managing your money. It can be overwhelming to start, and the financial industry does you no favors either. Financial professionals are notorious for using jargon, and it might give you a headache just to talk to them. And you wouldn't be alone: as many as one-third of women report that their financial advisers are patronizing.[1]

But you can take simple steps to manage your money. You don't have to figure it all out at once. If you commit to adding one new money habit every month, you'll be on your way to managing your finances like a pro.

Set financial goals

Here's something you can start with: commit to regularly laying out your financial goals. In chapter 9, you defined your values. So how do you translate those values into goals? Consider what is important to you. What do you want to achieve financially? What will make you feel like your money was put to good use?

Here are three examples of goals you might set:

1   Save for a trip to Hawaii.

2   Save for child's education (Registered Education Savings Plan (RESP) in Canada; 529 plan in the US).

3   Max out contributions to TFSA (Canada) or Roth IRA (US).

Once you have a few basic goals, add details such as dollar amounts and timelines for achieving them by.

1   Save $5,000 over eighteen months for a trip to Hawaii.

2   Contribute $2,500 each year to child's education fund.

3   Contribute $6,000 per year to max out TFSA/Roth IRA.

Writing down your goals, financial or otherwise, makes you 1.2 to 1.4 times more likely to achieve them.[2]

Pay yourself first

I'm pretty sure this is the golden rule of personal finance, and it's so ubiquitous I don't know who first came up with it. It's a good habit that you should implement as soon as possible. Paying yourself first means that as soon as you are paid—whether from a nine-to-five job or a freelance gig or a side hustle or even if you receive a cash gift—you put away a portion of that money for your future self. Rather than waiting until the end of the month to see what money is left over, you set it aside for you and your goals first. Using the goals in the example above, you would need to pay yourself the following:

1   $278/month to Hawaii trip fund (to save $5,000 in eighteen months)

2   $208/month to child's education savings fund (to contribute $2,500 a year)

3   $500/month to TFSA/Roth IRA (to reach the maximum allowable limit of $6,000 a year)

Put yourself first. It will make all the difference.

Automate

We've already talked about automating your monthly bill payments and money transfers, and I can't recommend this approach enough. Depending on your pay schedule, you can set up monthly, biweekly, or weekly automatic transfers and payments. Using our example goals, if you are paid biweekly (on the fifteenth and at the end of each month), you would set up transfers for the sixteenth and first of each month:

1   For the trip to Hawaii: $139 ($278 divided by 2) transferred into a special savings account

2   For the child's education: $104 ($208 divided by 2) paid to that fund

3   For the TSFA/Roth IRA: $250 ($500 divided by 2) transferred to that account

For longer-term savings goals, such as for children's education or retirement, move this money into a brokerage account that is set up to purchase mutual funds, stocks, or bonds. These generally provide a much higher rate of return than a standard savings account. (We'll talk more about investing in chapter 19.)

Money dates

Set aside time at least once per month (ideally twice, if you are paid twice a month) to check in on your finances. This will give you a good understanding of the items that you purchase regularly, and over time, you will get a better view of your spending habits and patterns. Here's a step-by-step ritual for your money date:

1   Prepare a beverage of choice (tea, coffee, wine).

2   Start with a review of your short- and long-term goals and costs.

3   Review your spending for the month.

4   Review your savings and investment contributions.

5   Note the current value of your investment accounts.

6   Calculate your net worth (see previous chapter).

7   Identify any expenses to cut.

8   Identify any bills that you could potentially lower or subscriptions you could cancel.

9 Decide what you will do with an increase in income or cash windfall.

If you share your financial life with someone, I recommend adding the following important step at the outset of your money date: promise your partner you will be judgment free (and have them do the same).

Plan your spending

If you have a big purchase coming up—for example, you know you're going to need to replace the furnace or you need to save up for a new-to-you vehicle—then plan for it. I'd encourage you to plan for your regular day-to-day spending too. Budgeting gets a bad reputation, but if you flip the narrative and refer to it as a *spending plan*, it's a lot easier to digest. Planning how much you're going to spend in the year is important; what's less important is making sure that you hit $450 per month on groceries. Prices, wants, and needs fluctuate—some months you'll spend $500 on groceries and others you might spend $400. It all evens out in the end.

When it comes to creating your spending plan, start with the savings and investment transfers you want to make. From there, I'd recommend outlining all of your fixed expenses (expenses that are the same every month) and then your variable expenses (things that change with usage). After that, include your discretionary spending for the month. Again, don't plan things down to the dollar, and leave some flexibility for overages from month to month. You can find an example spending plan at pinktaxbook.com/ resources.

Allowing for fluidity in your spending plan will ensure you are not obsessing over every dollar each month. That's not what you want. Your money is a precious resource, and a limited one. By planning where you'll spend, you'll get the best emotional and financial return on your hard-earned dollars. I really don't care if you spend $100 at Starbucks per month—that could be of great value to you—what I do care about is that you don't spend $30,000 in a year when you were only planning on spending $20,000.

Commit to continuous education

When it comes to your money, there is always more to know. You don't have to know it all, and you certainly don't have to know it all right now. But if you commit to continuous learning, you will build your financial brainpower and "take back the bank"—you will become one more woman in control of her money and furthering the cause of financial feminism. Listen to podcasts (shout-out to the podcast I produce with Tara Faria, *The Pink Tax*), read books, take courses. There is so much to learn, and it's fantastic that you are taking this step—so keep it up! Check out the resources I've collected at pinktaxbook.com/resources.

14

DISASTER-PROOF
YOUR FINANCES

B Y NOW, I'm sure, like me, you are tired of talking about the global pandemic. What was supposed to last only a couple weeks, maybe even a month or two (lol), has at the time of this book's publication dragged on for more than three years. The pandemic has taken so much away from all of us, but it has hit marginalized groups the hardest. So many women have left the workforce. US Representative Katie Porter put it best: "Women. Accounted. For. All. The. Losses."[1]—and she's right. One in five American women has left the workforce since the pandemic started to take on caregiving responsibilities.

The pandemic has exacerbated just how much unpaid work women do. Whether picking up a child from school because they were exposed to a positive case, homeschooling, or caring for a sick or elderly parent, women have been expected to do it all. Since the pandemic started, women have increased their care work to more than four hours a day, while men's care work averages under two hours a day.[2] Women have seen an increase in their caregiving work and housework, while simultaneously seeing a decrease in support services.

For many women, the disruptions that began in 2020 led to giving up full-time paid work and taking on part-time work instead. As we've discussed, part-time jobs typically mean lower hourly wages, more precarious work, and lower (if any) benefits. It doesn't stop there: the losses compound the longer a woman is out of the workforce. For every year a woman who earns $60,000 a year is out of the workforce, she loses $200,000 over her lifetime—in lost wages, lost wage growth, and lost benefits.[3]

During the pandemic, women with young children were overwhelmed trying to homeschool and maintain full-time work, if they even had the option of working remotely. Of the people employed in five C roles (caring, clerical, catering, cashiering, and cleaning), 56 percent are women; women make up 82 percent of health care workers, 59 percent of educational instructors, and 59 percent of accommodation and food staff. These industries were hit the hardest, with a million jobs lost in Canada alone in March 2020. Of that one million, 63 percent were women— and as we look at the economic recovery, women have only recouped half of the jobs lost.[4]

To add insult to the injury, 34 percent of employed men with kids received promotions while working remotely compared to 9 percent of employed women.[5] It is curious to me how face-to-face time was always such an important aspect of being promoted and yet once we were all forced

A basic income for all would ensure that those who **cannot work have financial stability.**

to be remote, it was still predominantly men who received promotions.

We also saw an increase in gender-based violence during the pandemic, which was exacerbated by job loss, food insecurity, disrupted routines, strains on mental health, and fear of the virus.[6]

A lot of these stresses could be relieved with a universal basic income. A basic income for all would ensure that those who cannot work have the financial stability to keep a roof over their head, put food on the table, and take care of their physical and mental health. We must also advocate for a care economy that accounts for social and material care, such as child- and elder care, household cleaning, and other chores.

If there's one thing the pandemic made clear on a personal level, it's that we all need to disaster-proof our finances. So, what can you do?

Draw up a will

Most people don't think they need one until they have children or until they amass a sizable chunk of wealth. But as soon as you have assets to your name, and certainly if you have any dependents, you need a will. You want to make sure that your dependents are taken care of and that your financial assets go to the people or charities that you deem important. If you're looking for a straightforward place to build a will in Canada, and if you don't have a complex situation, Willful is a wonderful tech company focused on democratizing end of life planning. Trust and Will is the

American equivalent, providing modern estate planning for all families. Properly planning for the worst will give you peace of mind.

Buy insurance

There are many different types of insurance including life, critical illness, and disability, all of which you may want to ensure you are properly protected. Knowing that you and your dependents will be safe and cared for financially if you are unable to work is key to building your financial house. A good rule of thumb for insurance is to cover ten times your income. I recommend staying away from whole life insurance and instead focusing on a term policy that covers your family. Each situation is unique, but it's very important to have enough to cover your outstanding debts (such as a mortgage) as well as the cost of living for you and your dependents until they reach a working age.

Build your credit score

Although you don't want to obsess over each point on your credit score or on every update to it, having a good score is important, should you need to access credit to make ends meet. Obviously, relying on credit isn't an ideal situation, but preparing yourself financially means making sure your credit score is in a good place. (See chapter 5 for more on credit scores.)

Plan a barebones budget

Calculating and creating a plan to spend the bare minimum is no fun at all, but knowing exactly how much you need to sustain yourself for a month is imperative for financial preparedness. You can use your total barebones budget figure to calculate your emergency fund (see below). Set out this plan so that you can easily adopt it if you need to in a pinch. Proper planning before an emergency means one less thing to think about in a time of overwhelm.

Set aside an emergency fund

Building an emergency fund should be one of your top priorities. Most Canadians are only $200 away from not being able to pay their bills,[7] which could be one extra trip to the grocery store. This number is quite alarming but not surprising. Before the pandemic, common wisdom said to save three to six months of living expenses for emergencies. I always recommend six to nine months for self-employed people. Access to cash is important, so I encourage you to save at least six months in a high interest savings account separate from your regular bank account, so there is no temptation to use this money on nonemergency items. Out of sight, out of mind.

Multiply your barebones budget by six and aim to sock that away. Start small, saving $15 to $30 per week, and slowly increase the amount as your spending plan permits.

By the end of a year, you'll have well over $1,000 saved, and in a few short years, you can turn this into a substantial five-figure emergency fund. Just $50 a week for four years is more than $10,000—and that's without interest.

Keep *some* cash on hand

By no means am I suggesting you keep thousands of dollars under your mattress, but in a world that continues to be more digital every day, we often forget that our technology could in fact go down. In 2022, a major internet outage[8] rattled many people and financial institutions. I was in Greece when this happened and had a number of credit cards go down—and I had very little cash on hand (okay, I had none). It became apparent very quickly just how reliant we are on technology. Keeping a couple hundred dollars in cash in a safe place in your home isn't a bad idea—just in case.

15

MONEY MINDSETS
AND MANTRAS

DON'T KNOW about you, but every once in a while I have a scarcity mindset that kicks in about money. *What if I get laid off? Do we have enough to live on if one of us isn't working? What if we get sick? Would we have to sell our house?*

I want to note that it is easy for me to educate women similar to me on money mindsets, but I cannot understand what it is like for those with generational trauma and the ongoing damage of colonization. In 2022, I enrolled in a course called the Trauma of Money,[1] which I'd recommend to anyone interested in unlearning capitalism. In it, we discussed how money memories impact our ability to financially function in society; we also deepened our understanding of how debt and intersectionality affect our mental health. I learned how money trauma (which many of us have—whether individual or generational) shapes our beliefs about money and our capitalist society.

At the best of times, we can slip into a scarcity mindset, but when catastrophe hits, many of us jump to the worst-case scenario. We fall into a vicious cycle that tells us we'll never have enough, even though in many cases our bank accounts are just fine. A scarcity mindset about your finances can hurt your happiness. You may find yourself unable to enjoy your earnings. Often, a scarcity mindset is exacerbated by not consciously being involved in your finances. So when things take a turn and you *must* look at your finances, you're completely overwhelmed. Learning about your money is easier when you're in a good financial position with no stress; it's a lot scarier when you're forced to no longer ignore it. Scarcity can also be driven by the money trauma you learned as a child from the behavior of the adults around you.

Investing in your money mindset and creating a healthy and positive relationship with your money are forms of financial self-care. Money is a tool, and you can't let it run your life. You can approach your finances from an abundance mindset instead. The objective here is to feel free to enjoy the money you've worked so hard to earn. This happens when you fully understand your financial situation and are able to work through the relationship you have with money.

An abundance mindset allows you to experience joy and gratitude for what you have and to know how much is enough. An abundance mindset allows you to be generous with others, without financial fear. It takes effort to get here, but it's worth it.

Our money mindsets are influenced early on.[2] The money stories we tell ourselves are the ones we learned as children. The way our parents handled money directly impacts how we manage and think about our own money. I was naturally very curious about money, but my parents didn't discuss it much. My sister and I were always taught to save money for a rainy day but not about investing, building wealth, or negotiating a salary. We weren't even allowed to *talk* about salaries. I was told I could find out what my parents earned once I was eighteen... and it was the first question I asked on my eighteenth birthday. But not having those conversations early on meant that I didn't think much about my money and spent it on whatever I wanted, without any discipline.

If you grew up in a home where there wasn't enough money for groceries, you may still believe that there will never be enough... no matter how much you earn. Conversely, money might have been used to solve all the problems in your household. Maybe your parents tried to buy your love, instead of addressing problems emotionally or intellectually. You might find yourself doing the same to those you care about most in your life.

So think about it. What is your first money memory? How does it affect how you relate to and manage money? Do you have a scarcity or abundance mindset? Can you unpack what experiences shaped it? If you have a scarcity mindset, you might always feel behind, as though bills and other payments are piling up. You might overschedule yourself at work or say yes to opportunities that aren't right for you because you are afraid another opportunity won't come.[3] If you have an abundance mindset, you can be present when you spend, be grateful for what you have, and be in control of your money life.

What is your first money memory? How does it affect how you relate to and manage money?

Of course, it is a lot easier to find gratitude when you are already well off.

If you have a scarcity mindset, you may need to figure out where that scarcity stems from and possibly work through some money trauma. A good therapist can help with this if you aren't sure how to tackle the damage that has been done. Beyond that, establishing good money habits and having a strong money mantra can flip your narrative about how you see and value your hard-earned dollars.

A money mantra

What is a money mantra, you ask? A money mantra is a short but powerful statement that you declare to yourself, either in your head or out loud, to become more confident with your finances. For example, whenever I am slipping into a scarcity mindset, my money mantra is *I will always be able to make more money.*

I repeat this mantra to myself when I'm feeling like we don't have enough saved or are spending too much. It isn't an excuse to spend every dollar that hits our bank account, but a reminder to set aside my fear of scarcity. Every money mantra should be personalized—it has to resonate with you. Reminding myself that I have the ability to earn more money allows me to focus on ways to increase my income rather than exist in scarcity.

A healthy money mindset facilitates living life on your own terms. You don't always have to have more money, but having an abundance mindset will make your life easier.

16

ASK FOR MORE

E'VE TALKED about how women are paid less than men—yes, the wage gap is real and it is perpetuated by the patriarchy. Negotiating is one way that women can combat salary disparities. Remember, earning less translates to saving and investing less, which ultimately leads to the wealth gap.

To narrow that wage gap and propel women forward financially, we need to negotiate. But we often find negotiating intimidating. There are so many studies out there that show women are perceived as aggressive or bitchy when we ask for more.[1] In my friend Fotini Iconomopoulos's book *Say Less, Get More,* she challenges everyone to think about how they negotiate every single day. It isn't only about asking for a higher salary. If you've ever asked for an upgrade when you're traveling, figured out who will do what chores in the household, or even collaboratively decided on a deadline at work, you have negotiated.

Women on average negotiate less. According to an article in *Forbes,* "Sixty-eight percent of women accepted the salary they were offered and did not negotiate, a 16-percentage point difference when compared to men (52%)."[2] This is troubling considering women already earn less and wages have been stagnant for the last thirty or so years. Our lack of negotiating makes it even harder for us to get ahead.

Negotiating at the beginning of a career has compounding effects for years to come. A $5,000 increase in salary at the beginning of a career equates to $750,000 in the full scope of a working life.[3] Just as your investments grow when you invest early and often, by kick-starting your earnings potential, you will see dividends well into your retirement years.

Asking good questions that make the party you are negotiating with stop and think is a great strategy. By using open-ended questions instead of yes-or-no questions, you can learn what is important to the other party, instead of giving away what it is you want. For example, you might say:

- "That salary is lower than I was expecting. Is there another way we can make up the gap?"

- "Are you flexible on other aspects of my compensation, such as bonuses, stocks, or vacation time?"

- "Based on my experience, I would expect to be paid within the range of $X to $Y. What can we do to get there?"

More vacation time, a signing bonus, variable pay, or work-from-home policies could be of value to you, and some negotiating points may be easier than others for an organization to grant.

When I negotiated my most recent position, the company I was leaving was going to require I pay them back

A $5,000 increase in salary at the beginning of a career equates to **$750,000 in the full scope of a working life.**

for some training I had done... to the tune of $6,000. I was really hoping that my new company would cover the cost. When I first asked, the hiring manager flat-out said no. I asked him if we could look at other options. Could he approve an increase to my base salary? Again no. The company was offering me a small signing bonus so I turned my attention there. Could the company increase this amount so that I could cover the repayment? He asked me for a number. I told him $6,000, and he grossed it up to $8,000 (to account for taxes, of course). Within hours, he called me back with an approved signing bonus for the $8,000—plus more. What had seemed like such a daunting chunk of cash to repay was something they were easily able to accommodate; it just had to be in the right terms.

Negotiating pays off whether it's at work, in your personal life, or when it comes to your expenses. You can literally negotiate anything, and on average people who negotiate end up being able to retire eight years earlier than those who don't. Fotini calculates that she'll retire at least twenty years early because of her negotiations![4] Isn't that amazing? Look around and find things you might be able to negotiate. Here are some places to start:

- **Salary.** Whether it's a starting salary, an annual raise, or a midcycle performance review, you have a lot of options of when to ask for an increase.

- **Vacation.** This is usually an easy one to negotiate when joining a new company. Many employers offer a lot of flexibility when it comes to vacation time.

- **Signing bonus.** The base salary for a specific position may be dictated by HR policy. When you can't increase the base, ask for a signing bonus to get more cash up front, especially if you have incurred expenses to take on this job.

- **Variable pay.** You can negotiate a higher variable pay, also known as long-term incentive or bonus pay, based on your base pay. It's always good to ask what percentage of individuals in the company receive their entire variable pay, as many employees may be surprised when they get 50 to 80 percent of the number outlined in the variable pay portion of the contract.

- **Company shares (equity).** If your company is publicly traded, make sure to negotiate for shares. In many cases, these stocks are vested over a three- or four-year period so you won't be getting the investment right away.

- **Parking and transportation.** You may be able to get your employer to cover your monthly parking and/or transportation costs.

- **Cell phone bill.** Calling your cell phone provider can be one of the lowest risk ways to start negotiating. In many cases, asking for more data or a better plan is a great way to lower your monthly costs. If you switch to a new provider, you can also ask for additional credit.

- **Credit card interest rate.** If you aren't paying your credit card off every month, it is worth your time to call your credit card company and ask them for a lower interest rate. This could save you a ton in interest payments over the long run.

- **Bank fees.** If you're being charged by your bank to use your checking account, ask for the fees to be reversed or for free banking. There are online banks out there that don't charge you anything to bank with them, and if you're willing to explore those options or tell your bank you feel its fees are too high, the representative will often try to do something to keep you as a customer.

- **Facebook Marketplace.** Another low-stakes way to build negotiation confidence is on Marketplace. If something is listed for $40, offer $30 and you'll likely meet in the middle at $35. If the seller won't budge, someone else will probably be selling the same item in a few days.

- **Vehicle.** Whether the vehicle is new or used, dealerships can lower the purchase cost. If the discount isn't off the original price, the dealership may be able to cover the shipping fee, the cost of your winter tires, or even maintenance for the first year.

- **Renovations.** While it can be hard to negotiate the overall price, you may be able to get extra service or an upgrade just by asking.

My aim for you is to step into your financial confidence by asking for what you want. So often we as women feel we can't do this, but it's important to remember that the worst thing you'll hear is no.

Happy negotiating!

17

FINANCIAL CONFIDENCE

ONFIDENCE IS not a fixed characteristic. It can be increased over the course of your lifetime. Think of when you were younger: you likely weren't as confident in some particular area, but you practiced that skill and became more confident your ability.

I grew up as a competitive dancer, and in eighth grade, I attended a month-long summer intensive at the Royal Winnipeg Ballet. Practicing ballet for six to eight hours a day, seven days a week, was unlike anything else that I've ever put my body through. I remember the very first class, surrounded by my fellow leotard-clad ballerinas, I stood at the barre for warmup and nearly collapsed when the instructor told us to extend one leg and hold it out, without any assistance from our hand, for a full song (about three minutes). Ten seconds in, my leg was trembling like it never had before. I felt weak and embarrassed, and we were required to do this every day. On the first day, my leg was about four inches off the ground by the end of the song and my entire body was shaking. If someone had asked me to do that on stage, I would not have had the confidence to do so. But fast-forward thirty days, and I could hold my leg up for the entire song, nearly at the height of my head. It would go on to become one of my signature moves in many of my routines for years to come. Practice makes perfect.

Money is not unlike dance in the sense that it takes a lot of practice and can be quite detailed. Being overwhelmed by the topic of finances just means you are at the beginning of your wealth-building journey. You're probably going to shake the first few times you exercise your money muscle, but after a while you'll be a pro. You may end up even discovering it's something you're really good at.

Women on average own fewer investments than men. They are less likely to buy stocks or become angel investors. For a long time, people assumed this was because women understood finances less than men. But as we dig into the data, we see a different reality. The study "Fearless Woman: Financial Literacy and Stock Market Participation" revealed that women tended to choose "do not know" when answering financial literacy questions. However, when the "do not know" option was removed, women chose the correct answers more frequently than men.[1] This highlights the fact that the investing gap is not about knowledge so much as it is about a lack of confidence.

Why do women have less confidence? Well, I'd argue that it has to do with:

1 Less experience
2 Less exposure
3 Conditioning

Let me explain.

Most people don't know what the hell they are doing when it comes to money as they first start out—but like anything, the more opportunity someone has to learn about something, the more confident they become. We have already discussed that women are less involved in financial decisions than men. They haven't become familiar with the financial jargon, and they aren't comfortable with it. Less exposure to money goes hand in hand with less experience managing it.

The gendered conditioning starts when little boys are told they are brave and courageous, and little girls are praised for being quiet, kind, and helpful. It's no wonder that boys grow up with more appetite for risk and more willingness to get involved in things they don't know much about. By the time girls get to high school, they speak up less than boys, and when they do, they aren't as confident. These trends extend to money matters.

So, we must watch how we speak to our children—especially our little girls—and we must include them in money decisions and conversations early and often. The more we talk about money openly and make space for women to ask questions, the sooner we will close the confidence gap.

Implementing financial literacy programs in school can also close the confidence gap.[2] If basic finances became a mandatory course, like math, social studies, or physical education, then most youth would graduate with some level of financial literacy. Starting these conversations early normalizes money and makes it easier for young women to ask money questions, and sets them on a path to build wealth.

18

INTERNALIZED CAPITALISM

S IDE HUSTLES and the gig economy have become integral parts of our life as millennials. I've always been a hustler, constantly finding ways to make additional income, always holding a number of jobs at any given time. I love a good side hustle because I believe that in many circumstances it can be easier to earn extra income than it can be to cut expenses. That being said, I fundamentally believe our society is broken when you *need* to work multiple jobs to afford "the game of life." If you're a single mom and need to work three part-time jobs just to put a roof over your head or food on the table, the problem is not you—it's the society we've built.

Internalized capitalism ties the worth of an individual to how productive they can be. You may worry that if you aren't working, you are lazy,[1] and many people end up putting their work before their mental health. With the "work hard, play hard" mentality in so many industries, it's no wonder we feel constantly pushed to do more. Internalized capitalism at its core is driven by white supremacy and pressures from inside families and social groups to conform. White men are rewarded for having corporate jobs that bill a lot of hours at a high rate, and everyone else is deemed as not quite as valuable because their work doesn't advance the profits of a large company.

For some people, there is time for side hustles—maybe younger individuals with few responsibilities—but as soon as you start throwing children into the mix, mental health challenges, or any number of circumstances, it can be impossible to work sixty-plus hours per week… and no one should have to.

Capitalism has tricked us into believing that our worth is tied to our ability to be productive; even though our society has become increasingly productive, workers have not seen any benefits. There is a constant push to work more than forty hours a week, despite the fact that practices such as four-day workweeks have been shown time and time again to increase happiness and productivity.[2]

If you find yourself in a scenario where you can take on extra work or sell your belongings on Facebook Marketplace or Poshmark, then it's a great practice to give that side-hustle stream of income a "job." The money you earn from tips as a server, selling used clothing, or writing online should have a specific purpose to give you a sense of satisfaction that those extra hours of work paid off.

You might use the money to reduce debt. Paying off a credit card, personal loan, or mortgage can be incredibly freeing! When you are debt-free, your money is 100 percent yours, you don't carry the burden of knowing you owe somebody, and you can spend it on whatever you want.

Investing is another great job for your money. Compounding returns will build a nest egg faster than simply saving—and this can be pretty inspiring. Watching the money you worked so hard for work hard for you back is a real boost.

19

WEALTH
BECOMES HER

I'VE MENTIONED the investment gap and how women tend to have less confidence but more knowledge than they think. Only four in ten women are comfortable with their investing knowledge; two-thirds of women don't feel comfortable making investing decisions; and 81 percent of women investors have experienced strong stereotypes about their investing acumen or financial status, according to the Capital Group.[1]

Here's a secret: women are better investors than men. It's true! In an interesting study called "Boys Will Be Boys"[2] (because of course it was), researchers studied 35,000 participants and found that women outperformed men in investing, because the men were overconfident and that led them to overtrade. Fidelity Investments found that women on average return 0.4 percent[3] more than men annually in their investment portfolios. That might not sound like much, but when we look at multimillion-dollar portfolios or billion-dollar funds, we're looking at hundreds of millions (if not billions) of dollars each year.

In addition to performing better, women also care more about socially responsible investing, with 55 percent of women prioritizing impact investing.[4] With gender impact exchange-traded funds (ETFs) and sustainability becoming more of a focus in the financial sector, it's easier than ever to use your money to make the world a better place.

Dear reader, your wealth becomes you, and one of the best ways you can build wealth is through investing—make your money work hard for you. You spend forty hours a week earning the cash that gets deposited into your bank account. You can't afford for that money to lose value sitting in cash.

A lot of people are scared of investing. They think that if they invest in the stock market, they could lose all their money. If you invest in a risky single stock (maybe a penny stock), yes, you could lose a lot of money. But if you understand what you're investing in, look for companies that provide long-term value, and ultimately build a well-diversified portfolio (more on this below), you don't have anything to worry about. I tell my students that if the entire stock market were to crash to zero tomorrow, then everyone subscribed to our financial system would have a lot bigger problems than the $5,000, $25,000, or even $100,000 we invested and lost. We would be back to the barter system as money would have absolutely no value.

Not investing is the most expensive mistake you can make in your lifetime.

Consider this scenario: you set aside $25,000 at the age of twenty-five and contribute an additional $5,000 per year until you are sixty-five. Your financial situation will look very different at retirement depending on your rate of return. If you kept your money in a savings account earning, let's say, 2 percent, you will have $363,000 when you retire. That's not bad, right?

But if you invest in a well-diversified portfolio that earns 8 percent, you will retire with $1.9 million.

Not investing would cost you more than $1.5 million over the course of your lifetime.

Can you imagine?

Experts suggest we will need around $2 million to retire, and thinking about saving $2 million seems incredibly daunting. But by investing your money, you only need to save $225,000 over the course of forty years.

If you're thinking, *Janine, an 8 percent return is insane,* I get it. I hear this all the time. But the average return of the stock market for the past fifty-plus years is around 10 percent per year—so that 8 percent is quite conservative.

When you start investing, you need to understand three things: where you're going to invest, what you're going to invest in, and "who" is going to invest.

Where you're going to invest

There are different investment accounts available to you depending on whether you live in the US or in Canada.

In Canada, your options are a TSFA and an RRSP (Registered Retirement Savings Plan).

TFSA (Tax-Free Savings Account)

A TFSA allows you to invest your after-tax dollars. The benefit of this account is that any growth you experience can be withdrawn tax free. This is your single best wealth-building asset as a Canadian, and it should be used for long-term retirement growth. Canadians can build a seven-figure TFSA by maxing out their contribution room and investing their money. You start accumulating contribution room the year you turn eighteen. An updated table of contribution room is on my website at pinktaxbook.com/resources, and it's also available on the Canada Revenue Agency (CRA) portal (though it is not always up-to-date).

If you have ever contributed to your TFSA before, you will need to subtract the amount that you have contributed from the amount of lifetime contribution room you have left. If you make a withdrawal from your TFSA, you can recontribute that amount as of January 1 of the following year.

Let's take the example of someone who was born in 1991 and has maxed out their TFSA contributions at $88,000 (2023 maximum). That individual invests within their TFSA, earning 8 percent, and if they never contribute any more money, in thirty-five years (when they are sixty-six) they will have $1.3 million in that account. The best part is that when they pull out that money, they don't pay *any* taxes, which ultimately means $303,278 in tax savings. That's right, had they invested this $88,000 in an unregistered account that isn't tax sheltered, when they retired and started using their investments to live off, they would owe $303,278.

The 2023 TFSA annual contribution amount was $6,500, which translates to $541 per month or $270 per biweekly paycheck. If you break it down this way, it can feel a lot more approachable to max out that contribution room.

RRSP (Registered Retirement Savings Plan)

An RRSP is a tax deferred account. What this means is that your contributions to it decrease your annual income taxes owed. RRSP contributions can even trigger a tax refund. You can use this money to recontribute to your investments if you're looking for more ways to grow your wealth. Similar to the TFSA, you will need to invest your money in this account to grow your wealth. The contribution limit is 18 percent of your earned annual income (and this amount can be found on your Notice of Assessment from the CRA), up to a maximum of $30,780 (2023). When you pull money out of your RRSP, you pay tax on it. The hope is that you will be in a lower income tax bracket when you pull money out than you were when you contributed.

Note that you don't need to claim your contribution on your tax refund the year that you make it; you can carry it forward until you are in a higher tax bracket (but not after age seventy-one).

There are two ways to pull money from your RRSP without triggering any tax—the Lifelong Learning Plan (LLP) and the Home Buyers' Plan (HBP; first-time buyers only)—but you need to pay the amount back over a predefined timeline.

Roth IRA and 401Ks

In the US, a Roth IRA is very similar to a TFSA, except the contribution room does not carry forward—if you don't

Not investing is the most expensive mistake you can make in your lifetime.

contribute the max amount in each year, you lose it. In 2023, the maximum amount you could contribute was $6,500 (or $7,500 if you were fifty or over).

The 401K is similar to the RRSP in that it is a tax deferred account. The maximum you could contribute if you were under fifty in 2023 was $22,500; if you were over fifty, you could contribute a catchup contribution of $7,500.

What you're going to invest in

You can make different types of investments. Through banks or investing firms, you can purchase:

- **Stocks.** A stock denotes ownership of a company. If a company has 100 shares (stocks) and you own one, then you own 1 percent of the company. Each stock trades at a price on the stock market, and you can buy or sell them. A stock is considered equity. If you buy at a lower price than you sell, you make a profit.

- **Bonds.** This is a type of fixed income; you are loaning a company money and in return they pay you a fixed interest rate.

- **Index funds.** These are portfolios of stocks and bonds that follow the performance of the stock market. Similar to stocks, you can buy and sell units of this fund on the stock market.

- **Exchange-traded funds.** ETFs are composed of a group of predefined companies. You can buy units of these funds on the stock market.

- **Mutual funds.** A pool of assets, similar to ETFs, that is actively managed by a fund manager (who usually charges a fee).

- **Cryptocurrency.** Digital or virtual currency that is traded and verified through the blockchain, essentially guaranteeing the fidelity and security of transactions.

Your goals and your appetite for risk are two factors that influence what you invest in.

Start simple by purchasing funds that are well diversified (meaning they're invested in lots of different things). ETFs are my favorite, and your bank may offer some of these. You may want to work with a financial adviser or portfolio manager to help you invest wisely. (We'll talk more about financial advisers in the next chapter.)

One of the biggest misconceptions about investing is that you need a lot of money to start. Well, I'm here to bust that myth. You need $25 to start investing—that's what I had when I started and you can absolutely do the same.

"Who" is going to invest

You have three options for who is going to invest your money for you:

1 Financial adviser
2 Robo adviser
3 You!

A financial adviser is someone who can make investments on your behalf. Depending on who this adviser works for, they may be limited to investing in certain funds, but they'll have access to stocks. While it can feel good to have a hands-off approach, at the end of the day, if you don't know what's going on with your investments, you could end up invested in things that don't align with your values or goals. A financial adviser also charges a fee, sometimes thousands of dollars per year, and may have a minimum balance requirement to take you on as a client.

A robo adviser is a digital platform that automates your investing based on your financial situation and goals. It gathers information about you through an online survey and then invests for you based your responses. Wealthsimple is one of my favorite robo advisers in Canada, and in the US, companies like Betterment and Acorns are available. These platforms do charge a fee, but these fees are substantially lower than what a financial adviser would charge. Robo advisers are a great place to get started.

Lastly, you can learn to invest your money yourself! I think absolutely everyone should learn how to manage their own investments so that they are in control of their financial future. If you're just getting started, there are low cost brokerages, like Questrade in Canada and Fidelity in the US. You'll likely want to start by investing in ETFs to build a well-diversified, low-risk portfolio. If you are interested in learning to do it yourself, I teach a six-week investing course (The Wealth Lab) that walks you through the entire process. You can find more information at pinktaxbook.com/resources.

When choosing who will do your investing, pay attention to fees. Your financial institution will charge fees to manage your investments. Look at the management expense ratio (MER): the lower this fee is, the better. You definitely want to choose one that is under 1 percent; I'd even say under 0.5 percent if you're just starting out. Fees absolutely eat into your long-term returns and can cost hundreds of thousands of dollars over a lifetime. The difference between a MER of 2.69 percent and 1.53 percent over the course of your lifetime is almost $60,000. A MER of 2.69 percent compared to a fund with a fee of close to 0 percent means paying $167,000 more in fees.[5] Investment fees are charged regardless of performance—if your investment goes down, the fee is still charged, which eats into your original amount, and makes it harder to build your wealth back up.

Lastly, contribute often. This is called dollar cost averaging (DCA), and it's important because we can't time the stock market. Believe me, if I could, I would be a very rich lady retired on a private beach. I generally encourage people to contribute once a month or more. Buying frequently is important to hit the highs and lows of the market. Stay consistent even when the market goes down, which it will. Remember you're in it for the long haul (think thirty to forty years). The general trend of the market is up!

20

WORTH LESS

AT TWENTY-SEVEN, Ashley wanted to start investing. She was new to the financial world but wanted to save for her education, future home, and retirement. To start her investing journey, she did what most of us do. She went to the bank where she had been a customer since she was thirteen. She thought to herself that they must know what they are doing: they just posted record-breaking profits. She felt confident that they would be able to help her. She was assigned a senior financial adviser and tried to ask questions during her appointment. Ashley was cut off over and over, as the adviser walked her through a risk profile questionnaire and enrolled her in a bunch of mutual funds she had no idea about. Like so many people, Ashley left this meeting feeling frustrated, overwhelmed, and confused. Over the coming days, she began to feel anxious. What exactly had the adviser pushed her to purchase? He really only seemed interested in making a sale (investments are what they sell, after all) and not in helping Ashley learn.

Women in North America are coming into a lot of money over the next decade, which means that they will be looking for ways to manage and grow their wealth. Many households choose to hire an adviser to make a financial plan and manage their investments. But the financial industry is built by men, for men.

It's pretty obvious that the financial industry is doing a disservice to women. Financial advisers treat women differently than men, as evidenced by the fact that 70 percent of women in the US[1] (80 percent in Canada[2]) leave their financial adviser within a year of their husband dying. In a New York Life Investments study, 40 percent of women[3] said that they were treated differently and felt ignored or dismissed by their adviser. The Boston Consulting Group found that women were stereotyped, sent dumbed-down materials, spoken to in demeaning ways, and not being taken seriously by their financial advisers.[4] If women feel they are not respected or in a safe space when talking to their financial advisers, it can create a huge problem and erode our confidence.

Many women have financial advisers who make decisions on their behalf, investing them in asset classes (a group of securities that are similar and behave similarly in the market) that aren't appropriate for their goals or stages of life. They might recommend a young woman invest in a portfolio of bonds (fixed income asset class) that has little opportunity for growth, or keep a woman near retirement invested in 100 percent stocks (equity asset class), which are far riskier than bonds.

Always remember, you are the one in charge of your financial life. If your financial adviser is rude or does not have your best interest at heart, fire them. I'm not a huge fan of financial advisers—I vehemently believe we can manage our money and build our wealth ourselves without all of the extra fees. But if you decide to use one, I want to give you the tools to ask money-smart questions. A financial adviser who understands you and your situation, does not speak down to you, and meets your goals and objectives should be table stakes. Unfortunately, this is harder to find than you'd hope, and not many women are in the finance profession.

If you decide to work with a financial adviser, look for someone who talks to you directly, asks questions about your preferred style of communication, and makes eye contact with you—especially if you have a husband and he is in the room too. Choose someone who is open about their fees. The following questions will help you evaluate if your financial adviser has your best interest at heart.

What types of investments do you put your client's money into?

Your adviser might invest in stocks, bonds, index funds, ETFs, or mutual funds, and that can have an impact on the returns you'll see and what level of risk you're comfortable taking on. While you don't need to be an expert on any of the above, you should know what they mean for your investment portfolio.

What type of returns do you typically see for your clients?

Some advisers will say this depends, which is totally understandable, but they should be able to give you a ballpark or average over the past number of years. They should be able to outline any swings they've seen in the market, and based on your age and risk profile, they should be able to give you an estimate on what you can expect.

How are you compensated?

Understanding how your adviser is paid is crucial. It could dictate what they invest your money in. For example, some advisers are compensated based on the number or type of funds they sell. If this is the case, they could push a fund on you that is more expensive to you, which benefits them. Fee-only financial advisers are typically the way to go. (Remember in chapter 4 when we covered biases?)

When you retire, what are your succession plans?

Some advisers are older than others, and if you're a millennial or younger, there is a good chance you're going to live longer than your adviser stays employed. It's important to ask this so that you know your money will be in good hands after your adviser steps away from work.

What is your investment approach and how do you decide on a good investment for a client?

Asking how your adviser chooses their investments is important even if you don't understand the nuances of their answer. Write down their answer and do some of your own research; it can be a great way to determine if they align with your investment values. If socially conscious investing (aka environmental, social, and governance, or ESG investing) is important to you, ask if they are an expert in this field. When the market goes down, do they have a stop-gap to minimize losses or are they going to focus on buying more?

How often do you contact your clients?

If you're the type of person who gets nervous when you hear about swings in the stock market, it will be important for you to have access to your financial adviser. A follow-up question to this might be about what method of communication they use.

Will I have access to my investment account online?

This may not be a big one for some people, but personally I like to be able to check on my investments monthly. Some people are perfectly content with receiving their quarterly statements. For people who don't want to actively manage their investments, an adviser can be a great way to go. Even if they are more expensive than purchasing your own portfolio, many advisers come with perks such as financial planning on an individual level.

PART

3

Support
New
Mothers

"Women will have achieved true equality when men share with them the responsibility of bringing up the next generation."

RUTH BADER GINSBURG

EVERY PERSON on this planet is born from a mother. And yet in so many times across history, we have devalued mothers and the unpaid work they do. Nothing speaks more strongly to this point than looking back to the 1960s when children were asked on school questionnaires what their parents did for a living and told to leave the line blank if their mothers were housewives.[1] Blank to signify the invisible, unpaid, underappreciated, and exploited work that women do all over the globe. We have placed higher value on the work men do outside of the home for centuries, but women's unpaid work subsidizes communities, countries, and men's careers. It's time we value women's unpaid work—and we can start with childcare.

21

AFFORDABLE, ACCESSIBLE CHILDCARE IS A MUST

W OMEN WHO live in countries that lack affordable and accessible childcare have some of the lowest levels of participation in the workforce.[1] Public, affordable, and accessible universal childcare is essential to women's economic empowerment and advancement.

There are currently 350 million children worldwide who need care and do not have access to it. While many of these children live in the global south, many also live in so-called developed countries (global north). The inflexibility and excessive cost of many childcare systems in the global north hinder women from participating in the workforce, which also affects their daughters' participation. Childcare centers, as well as home-based care, need to have flexible funding models and extended hours to meet the demands of our society[2] and support women in all careers, not just those in traditional nine-to-five jobs. There are many great examples of this kind of flexible childcare system worldwide, and we should look to these examples to see how to implement an appropriate and supportive system for all women in our own countries.

In Belgium, after-school care and care centers for smaller children are open from 7 a.m. to 6 p.m. and cost one euro per day. In France, nurseries for two-to-six-year-olds are free, and in Belgium, Denmark, Lithuania, Norway, and Slovenia, care for children under the age of three is also free. As of writing this, Canada is working on implementing $10 per day daycare across the country, following in the footsteps of the province of Quebec, which has had $7 per day daycare for decades. Some of its childcare centers are open twenty-four hours a day. We have started to see a decrease in the overall cost across Canada, but we still aren't where we need to be. For example, as part of the federal government's cost reduction strategy, Whitehorse, Regina, Ottawa, and St. John's were the only cities on track to meet the $20 per day goal for 2022.[3]

There are still challenges with accessibility in Canada.[4] As a new parent, I had to join a waitlist for daycare in our neighborhood when I was four months pregnant, and there was a spot open for my son when he was almost two years old. Now I don't know about you, but I could not take twenty-two months off work, nor did I want to. I went back to work at fourteen months, and even that was a stretch.

Affordability is key for childcare, and the US Department of Health and Human Services advises that childcare costs

Childcare is a
basic need.

should amount to no more than 10 percent of household income (otherwise it becomes prohibitive); however, the Organisation for Economic Co-operation and Development (OECD) reports that 15 percent of a family's net income is the average paid for childcare. New Zealand, the United Kingdom, and the US have the most expensive childcare in the world, spending an average of 36 percent, 29 percent, and 19 percent, respectively, of a two-parent family's net income on childcare.[5]

In addition to affordability, accessibility is key. In Canada and the US, there are daycare deserts[6]—places with no licensed local daycare, limiting the choices parents have. This compounds the issue as parents must commute to their childcare and then to work, if it's possible at all to find care.

Childcare is a basic need that governments around the world should fund to increase women's employment and productivity, create new jobs, improve child outcomes, and drive economic growth. But we often hear the other side of the argument on social media:

- "Universal childcare is too expensive to fund."
- "Who will pay for it?"
- "What about people who don't have kids—why should they pay?"
- And my favorite: "If you can't afford kids, don't have them."

But universal, affordable, and accessible childcare pays for itself. Employing more people to work at the childcare centers and paying them a living wage—that is, an income that allows individuals and families to afford adequate food, shelter, and other necessities—means they pay more taxes. Women returning to the workforce also means more tax revenue.

Children—future taxpayers—keep our economy in symbiosis over the long term. Without children, we won't have a next generation to be our doctors, lawyers, or baristas. The United Nations has stated that the current replacement rate—the number of children a family needs to have to maintain our current global population[7]—is 2.1. Each family must have 2.1 children to sustain the global population. In many developed countries, the rate is less than that, meaning we may see a population decline in certain countries. If a population ages and is not replaced, the burden to pay for health care and pensions, for example, grows.

Canadians decided that our society supports and pays for things like health care and infrastructure for most of its citizens. I say *most* because there are many northern and Indigenous communities that don't have access to clean drinking water and proper roads, for example. In this country, we don't turn to people who have cancer or need a hip replacement and say, "Well, I don't have to deal with those ailments, so why should I have to contribute to the cost of them?" I suppose some people do think that way, but the majority of us see the benefit in working together to cut costs by sharing them, bringing basic needs to as many people as we can. If you believe in women's equality in the workforce and the world, childcare should be treated no differently than health care, roads, or drinking water. We need to abolish the Pink Tax that we place on our mothers, particularly our new mothers. Ultimately, we need to build a care-led economy—one that values care work and acknowledges that it will play an important role in driving economic outcomes in the future.

22

PARENTAL LEAVE
PENALTIES

O
NE OF the most important aspects of supporting
parents in a financially feminist society is providing adequate maternity and parental leave, and it's
important to define the difference. Maternity leave
is the portion of the time off work that is strictly for the
medical recovery of the person giving birth. This leave
should be used for healing from what for many is a medical trauma, sometimes involving major abdominal surgery.
Parental leave is for either parent to use to care for the new-
born. In many countries around the world, parental leave
is predominantly taken by the person who gave birth; however, an increasing number of partners are splitting it.

Maternity and parental leave have been around for a
long time, but most countries don't give people with new
babies the time and money they deserve to raise their
new human. In 1919, the International Labour Organization created the Maternity Protection Convention, which

allotted six weeks of leave for women[1] after giving birth. It was updated in 1952 and states that twelve weeks should be the minimum of time off for maternity leave and women should not be paid less than two-thirds of previous earnings.[2] But many countries around the world offer twelve weeks off but don't pay for it. For instance, in Canada, the maternity portion of the leave is fifteen weeks. Check. However, the maximum amount you could receive from the government in 2023 was 55 percent of your earnings, up to $650 per week. The most you could receive in a month was $2,600, which is barely a living wage in most cities across the country. The US is even worse, only protecting twelve weeks, all of which are unpaid. It's worth noting that these payments, like many others, haven't been indexed to inflation.

After a maternity or parental leave, returning to work can be extremely overwhelming. So many changes can take place while you are on leave. You may have a different team, a different boss, maybe even different technology to learn. On top of all this, many mothers have an additional mental load—the cognitive effort involved in managing your work, relationships, a family, and a household[3]—when returning to work. Protecting women as they reenter the workforce is imperative.

When women return to the workforce, they are hit with the motherhood penalty. What's the motherhood penalty, you ask? It is the systemic disadvantage that women encounter in their careers after becoming a mother.

A loss of continuity in employment hurts women through a loss of seniority, reduced pension, and a reduction in paid annual leave benefits. Once a woman becomes a mother, she is passed over for opportunities and promotions more often than before she had a child. The motherhood penalty has been identified as 4 percent less pay per child.[4] In a 2019 study that aimed to quantify the motherhood penalty, it was found that in the US after ten years, a mother was earning 40 percent less[5] than before she gave birth. In Germany, it was 61 percent; in Denmark, 21 percent.

Women are seen as givers and caretakers. They are perceived as less serious about their careers once they have children. And it doesn't stop there. The motherhood penalty is deeply rooted in unconscious bias—women with children lose when compared to child-free men. Global Women, a diversity and inclusion organization, points out that women with children are held to a higher level of scrutiny for their actions.[6] Research shows that in Western nations, mothers are perceived as 10 percent less competent and 12 percent less committed to their jobs than women who are not mothers.[7] It was also found that women who talk about their children in the workplace are seen as more distracted[8]—compared to fathers who talk about their children being perceived as caring dads. This plays into the fatherhood benefit: men are still viewed as the primary breadwinners, and once they have children, they see a 6 percent increase in their wages.

Although 120 countries around the world provide paid maternity leave, some restrict how many leaves you can take and how often. In Nepal, the maximum number of leaves you can take is two. In Barbados, Egypt, Jamaica, and Zimbabwe, it is capped at three. In the Bahamas and

Tanzania, women are only allowed a mat leave once every three years. Often there are minimum lengths of service to qualify for a maternity leave, which therefore excludes many part-time workers or women with back-to-back pregnancies. In Switzerland, you need to work for three months to qualify for leave. In Egypt and the Philippines, six months is the minimum. Australia, New Zealand, and the United Arab Emirates require one year of service. By far the worst, Zambia and Gambia require two years before you can qualify for any type of leave.[9] This withholding of financial resources hurts women when they are at their most vulnerable—after giving birth with all the physical healing as well as the care for a helpless infant.

Paid leave improves both maternal physical and mental health and increases female employment in private firms. Adequate maternity leave also leads to lower infant mortality and an increase in breastfeeding, which has many physical and mental health benefits for babies and mothers.

Thankfully, several countries are moving in the right direction. By far my favorite country when it comes to parental leave, Sweden provides parents with 480 days of leave to use before the child turns eight. This offers amazing flexibility to parents who may need to take time off to care for a child when they cannot go to school, when they are sick, or when there's another emergency.

Although supporting new moms is key, one of the best ways we can close the gender wage gap is by having men take parental leave. In the EU, only 10 percent[10] of fathers take leave, and the number is even lower in North America. Countries that are leading the way in rates of men taking parental leave (Norway, Sweden) see success when men on leave are paid at a high percentage (greater than 70 percent) of their base salary and given use-it-or-lose-it leave that cannot be transferred to another parent.[11] When fathers take leave, it increases earnings for moms, decreases mother absenteeism, and allows fathers to build relationships with their children. There also tends to be a shift in the unpaid labor at home. Men start to see childrearing and domestic work as the responsibility of both parents.

When both men and women are expected to take time away from work to raise children, we don't see the same bias against women's compensation and promotion. If all people are equally as likely to take a parental leave, the bias starts to dissipate.[12]

What can you do?

While the world isn't where we need it to be yet when it comes to supporting paid leave for all parents, there are some things you can personally do to prepare yourself for a maternity or parental leave.

Save when you can

If you plan to have children one day, open a savings account and start transferring $25 or $50 per paycheck into it. Even if your leave is years away, these small sums of money will add up and build a nest egg for the costs of pregnancy and motherhood.

Save during your pregnancy

Remember that you have nine whole months to build up a bit of a buffer—especially if you're self-employed. It can be stressful and daunting to think about all of the new expenses you're going to face, along with a reduced income, while you're on leave. Remind yourself that you have time to save and that will hopefully put your mind at ease a little bit.

Pay into your plans on leave

If you can afford to pay into your benefits and retirement plans while you are on leave, then do so. This will allow you to continue to build wealth and benefit from employer matching (if your organization offers it), which is ultimately free money.

In the first year of your baby's life, it is likely that both of you are going to need follow-up medical appointments and potentially additional care. If you can keep your benefits while on leave, it could save you thousands. I personally needed a lot of chiropractor and massage therapy appointments, in addition to pelvic floor physiotherapy, after I gave birth. My son had a tongue and lip tie, and we chose to have it released by a dentist, which would have cost us over $500 if we had to pay out of pocket. Thankfully, our benefits covered it. Add to this the cost of mental health support, which I believe all mothers should have access to.

Pay off high interest credit cards

Credit cards can have extremely high interest rates, often costing people hundreds of dollars each month if they don't pay off the balance. (I consider anything higher than

8 percent too high, but such low interest credit cards can be hard to find.) If you have the ability to pay high interest cards off before the baby comes, your cash flow will be in a more positive position.

It's okay to scale back

There is so much pressure on new parents, and the last thing you need to worry about while you're on a reduced income is keeping up with all your savings goals. This may seem counterintuitive, but I want to give new parents a break. If you have to scale back on your retirement contributions or other savings goals while you're on leave, barely earning a living wage, it's okay. Give yourself some grace. It's a short period in your life and not worth the stress you'll put yourself through. So take a breath, it's going to be okay financially.

23

FOR RICHER
OR POORER

MOST PEOPLE aren't comfortable talking to their significant other about their finances, which is unfortunate because fights about finances are the number one cause of divorce. Money issues in relationships can be extremely tricky, especially if one person earns more—in many cases this causes the power dynamic to shift. In heterosexual relationships, it is still more likely for the man to be the primary earner, which is problematic when a couple looks at how to split money, who controls it, and what value is assigned to unpaid labor within the home.[1] Often women in such situations assume more of the unpaid household and care work, the financial value of which is not always considered. If a woman lacks financial control in a relationship, she may feel or be unable to make money decisions without approval from her spouse.

When I was eighteen, I worked in retail and often heard women calling their husbands for approval before purchasing a $200 bag. I'm not saying you shouldn't check in about large purchases with your partner, but it's good to have these conversations and thresholds set beforehand. To me, it seemed humiliating when women who so obviously wanted to buy the bag were denied permission by their husbands. These dynamics can be a slippery slope to financial abuse within a relationship.

We've talked about how if women around the world were paid minimum wage for all their care work, we would add $12 trillion[2] to the global economy. This figure shines a light on just how much unpaid care work women are doing as they support men's careers and uphold our communities.

If we want equality, we must assign value to all the resources within our households, monetary and otherwise. Women on average complete twenty-one more hours per week of unpaid work[3] than men. If we were to assign a monetary value of $25 per hour to this work, that would be an additional $2,100 a month ($27,300 per year). This is work that women perform over men in addition to their full-time jobs, and it doesn't even begin to scratch the surface on all the jobs that women do. In 2021, Salary.com identified that stay-at-home moms do eighteen different jobs (what!) and should be compensated US$184,820 annually.[4] It is completely wild to put a monetary value on the work that for hundreds of years has largely gone unnoticed. When we start to look at numbers like this, it's no wonder some men want women at home—they likely couldn't afford hiring for all eighteen of those jobs. Women's invisible unpaid labor upholds men's careers.

Divorce is pretty much one of the worst things a woman can experience financially, with one in five women falling into poverty because of divorce.[5] Approximately one out of every three women who owns a home and has children loses the house after divorce. One of the main reasons for this is that women take on more of the caregiving roles than their ex-husbands and don't receive their full child support payments.[6] In fact, 56 percent of custodial parents did not receive full payment of child support from the child's second parent,[7] meaning they are raising and paying for the majority of their children's upbringing, even though the child belongs to both parents.

Even before divorce, in heterosexual relationships, women's money tends to be assigned to pay for things such as childcare, vacation, and summer camp, which positions it as secondary, less relevant. A woman may be expected to direct her entire paycheck toward childrearing, while men often keep more disposable income for themselves. We often expect women to compare their salaries with the monthly cost of childcare. I'm sure many of us have had conversations with friends about exactly this—perhaps we've even been the one considering whether to go back to work because our after-tax paychecks will barely cover the cost of childcare. But the child belongs to both parents, so why do we tend to compare these costs only to the mother's pay?

In a partnership, both incomes should go toward the basic needs of the household, such as the mortgage, utilities, groceries, and childcare. But if you only look at your own paycheck relative to the cost of childcare, you and your partner are implying that it is your sole responsibility to care for the children. This kind of thinking can lead to women leaving the workforce at an alarming rate. A better way to think about this is to proportionally compare both partners' income to the total household earnings.

Seventy-four percent of millennials say they are stressed about money,[8] and yet there are astonishing statistics about how little partners want to commit to understanding each other's financial situations. Nearly 40 percent of individuals in relationships don't know what their partner earns.[9] Couples who fight about money and who have on average $30,000 in consumer debt, while also lacking assets, increase their chance of divorce by 70 percent.[10] These statistics show us that money plays a very real role in marriage, with 54 percent of people believing a partner with debt is a reason to consider divorce.[11] Talking about money and how you'll manage it together is one crucial way you can decrease the risk of divorce.

Earning more money also reduces the risk of divorce. Households with an income of more than $90,000 per year were found to be 13.5 times happier in their marriages than those with an income of $30,000. The chance of divorce decreases by 30 percent in households with more than $50,000 of income per year.[12]

Women live longer on average than men do, so it's important to share the role of chief financial officer managing money in the household. I've seen far too many women leave their retirement plans to their husbands, and if the worst happens (death or divorce), they are reeling in hurt while simultaneously piecing their financial situation together.

If you're in a relationship, what can you do so that you don't end up down this path?

Talk about money early and often

A couple of dates in, talk about money. Whether it is how you want to split the bills or what you want to achieve in the next couple years, a sense of your partner's financial priorities early on is important.

Discuss your values and spending styles

Once you've decided to invest in the relationship for the foreseeable future, you want to understand what financial values you each hold. Are you are spenders or savers? These conversations will help you both prioritize what to do with your shared resources.

Manage the household finances together

If you've decided to live together, you need to sort out how you're going to manage the finances, just like you would sit down and decide how you're going to raise your children. I've outlined above why it's imperative that both individuals be involved and that your income isn't seen as secondary. There are three ways you can split your finances.

You can *combine everything*, which is probably the easiest way to do things: both paychecks go into one account and all the expenses are paid out of this account. You'll need to be really clear on how much each person is able to spend from the joint account and what your financial priorities are.

Or you can *keep everything separate*. In this case, each person is responsible for their half of the bills in the household but everything else remains independent. One challenge with this approach is that, if you aren't on the same

We must assign value to all the resources within our households, **monetary and otherwise.**

page, you might one day discover you've gone in different directions altogether. For example, one person might be a super saver, ending up with millions in retirement, while the other, a spender, has nothing to show for themselves when they are old and gray.

Or you can do *proportional representation*. In this scenario, couples keep a joint account for bills and other expenses, and each person contributes an amount based on the percentage of the household income they earn. For example, the expenses may be split 60/40 or 65/35.

I've seen all three of these approaches work—as long as there is open and honest communication. Keeping everything separate is probably the best way to protect yourself from financial abuse and infidelity. A few of my friends who have been through divorce say they will never share bank accounts with their significant others again—and although this is anecdotal, I can imagine that unweaving that financial web you create together as a couple is a huge headache.

Have a will and insurance

Although this isn't the first conversation you think of once you get serious with someone, it's a really important one. Make sure that your financial assets will go to the person you want them to and that you're properly insured should tragedy strike.

Raising the next generation

Our money stories will shape who our children become as adults and their relationships with money. So, we need to

be mindful of how we raise our children—the next generation of financial feminists. In general, our society tells boys
money stories of abundance, strength, and power while
girls are taught scarcity and weakness. The media perpetuates this, using different language to speak to women than
they do to men. The articles written for men are usually
about investing hacks to make you rich. The narrative for
women is about cutting spending so that you can afford to
save. Take as just one example the headline for this *Cos-
mopolitan* article from December 2022: "38 Inexpensive
Clothing Websites That'll Go Easy on Your Wallet."

We have to be careful of the wage gap creeping into
how we raise our children—a study on allowances found
on average boys' allowances were $13.80 per week and
girls received just $6.71.[13] The perpetuation of the patriar-
chy runs deep and starts young. But if we are aware and
correct these behaviors, we can break the cycle for the generations to come.

Financial infidelity and abuse

Financial infidelity is hiding vital financial information and
transactions from your partner, and *financial abuse* is using
money to limit and control your partner's actions and freedom of choice[14]—and both are much more common than
people would like to think.

Forty-three percent of married Americans have undis-
closed credit card debt, and 51 percent of millennials have
committed financial infidelity.[15] Let me emphasize that:
half of millennials have lied to their partner about money.

This isn't a great habit to get into for obvious reasons—it could definitely lead to a lack of trust and the ultimate demise of the relationship. However, in situations of abuse, a woman may need to commit financial infidelity to get out of the relationship.

Money has and continues to be a way that men control women. This isn't a light topic, but my hope is that in sharing some of these statistics you might be able to recognize and help someone escape a situation that is unsafe or unhealthy. Ninety-nine percent of domestic violence cases involve financial abuse, and 85 percent of abused partners who leave eventually return to their abuser because of financial difficulties.[16]

Until we have proper social systems set up for women experiencing abuse, they will continue to go back to their abusers because they need to pay the bills. The Netflix show *Maid* (based on a book by the same name) depicts the experiences of author Stephanie Land and shows this dynamic playing out. We see how little money the main character, Alex, has and the choices she has to make to provide for her and her daughter's most basic needs. Her boyfriend cuts off her access to money by taking away her debit card. This harrowing story is the reality for so many women.

Red flags for financial abuse

What red flags should you look for to ensure you're not a victim of financial abuse? DC's Legal Aid Society outlines a few key signals that indicate that you may be in a situation of financial abuse.[17]

Interfering with work

This involves your partner telling you where you can or can't work; getting you in trouble by calling, texting, or showing up at your work all the time; keeping you from getting to work by, for example, taking your car without asking or "losing" your keys; or saying they will be on childcare duty and then not showing up.

Forcing you into debt

A financially abusive partner may run up charges on credit cards or open new accounts and credit cards in your name, saying they will pay the bills and then never doing it; pressure you into signing for things; and/or make you prioritize spending on family obligations while they buy things for themselves.

Calling all the shots

In this situation, you never know what resources your partner has or what's happening with shared money. You don't get to see bank accounts that you own or share and are kept on an "allowance"; you must ask permission to buy things you need or to show receipts for every dollar you spend. A financially abusive partner may also hold back money for things you or your children need, such as medicine or food.

Manipulating you with money

In this power imbalance, only one person ever pays for meals, gifts, and travel. They pressure you to "pay them back" for such spending with obedience, affection, or only give you money if you have sex with them. They might sabotage your other relationships by stealing money from your family or friends; tell you that you have no financial resources; or threaten that you'll be homeless without them.

Messing with benefits and legal threats

In this scenario, your partner may make you hand over public benefits (such as food stamps) or threaten to report you to benefits programs for cheating, even if you haven't done anything wrong. They may refuse to pay child support or say they'll never pay child support. They may drag out a divorce case to cause financial suffering, or threaten to do so.

If you find yourself nodding your head to one or more of these examples, you may be in a financially abusive relationship. If you are, please know you are not alone. So many people around the world have been through this. If it's safe to do so, confide in someone you trust, and explain your situation and your desire to get out of the financially abusive relationship. Ask a friend or trusted family member to set up a savings account for you so that you can start to build up an "escape fund" that can help you get out of this position. And where possible, seek professional help for your financial and mental well-being.

PART

4

Vote for Your Daughters

"We need a global under-standing that we cannot implement change effectively without women's political participation."

MEGHAN,
DUCHESS OF SUSSEX

THE ONLY WAY women can truly function as equals to the men in our society is if they are equal financially. Having the same financial power and leveraging it will allow us to take more leadership positions globally and change policy to aid in creating equity around the world. Financial feminism allows us to do that. It means everyone is equal in all aspects of their finances: what they are paid, their credit scores, and their ability to manage their ever-growing wealth. If we stay on our current trajectory, women's financial equality is more than 250 years away, which is way too far off. My hope is that after reading this book, you'll have both hope and tangible policies you can advocate for in your communities, corporations, and countries.

24

NO JUSTICE WITHOUT GENDER JUSTICE

MY HUSBAND often attends the Women's Global Leadership Summit with me. I sit on the planning committee for the conference, which brings six to seven hundred CPAs from Canada and the US together each year. One year, he was sitting in a session in which they had participants break into groups to brainstorm how we could work toward gender equality. When it came time for my husband to speak, he only said two words: "Vote better." The table was silent, stunned. It was 2018 and no one there had considered the possibility that who you vote for and their policies greatly impact gender equality in our society. We've been told for so long not to talk about politics, money, or sex; I imagine it's ingrained in most of our minds that who we vote for does not directly impact society's perception of us as a whole human being. He went on to say that being a woman in itself is political, and until we stop legislating women's bodies, when we talk about equality, we must talk about policy.

We've already discussed many aspects of financial feminism, but one of the most important things that will improve women's status is a change in policies around the world. And we need to do this quickly to ensure that we move toward equality and fairness in our society. We can advocate for our countries to implement financially feminist policies on the global stage; things like investing in education to increase literacy rates and transferring cash are ways we can help low-income countries build up an educated workforce that can afford the basics and continue to support women in the workforce.

In higher income countries, we can advocate for changes in tax systems to better benefit women. We need to shift from a family to an individual system for taxes and government benefits, because currently being in a couple has more advantages than being single. In Canada, we pay less taxes and receive more from the government (in most situations) if a family has two adults. This disproportionately harms single women who are often at the lowest end of the income spectrum.

Because families receive benefits for a lower income spouse, in many situations the woman stays as the lower earner or earns no income so that the family can take advantage of tax breaks. Keeping women in low-paying or no-pay roles perpetuates the wage gap. Nixing these tax rules will increase the number of women in the workforce.

Achieving gender parity requires us to recognize that every policy, program, and project affects men and women differently. It's not until we dig into the nuances that we will truly understand what needs to change. Policies must shift to compensate for the historical and systemic disadvantages that women have been subject to for centuries.

The European Institute for Gender Equality has put together a checklist for legislation to ensure gender equality,[1] and the OECD produced the *Toolkit for Mainstreaming and Implementing Gender Equality.*[2] Sweden has started to focus on gender-based budgeting to unpack how direct and indirect taxes affect men and women differently. One example is user fees.[3] Women are much more likely to be affected by user fees, such as transit costs, because in general they are more likely to use such services. Any increase to such fees is a direct hit to women's bank accounts.

Belgium has a gender test[4] that assesses the impact of regulation proposals on women and men. Portugal dictates that political parties must have gender quotas for their single/lower house at the subnational level.[5] If they fail to meet these gender quotas, they can lose anywhere from 25 to 80 percent of their funding. Imposing fines and taking away funding is punitive, but until we create actual consequences, we won't start to see the unraveling of the patriarchal systems ingrained in our societies.

Oxfam has created a helpful list of six policies for equity.

1. Invest in national care systems

Oxfam isn't only talking about childcare, though it does suggest at least fourteen weeks of paid maternity leave and one year of paid parental leave (use it or lose it). Care systems also include water, sanitation, pensions, and benefits for all people in our society. Raising the lowest common denominator makes our society stronger. Our governments

We can collectively elect people who **advocate for financially feminist policies.**

need to do this on a federal level. Doing so will ensure that we see an increase in demand for women's labor.

2. End extreme wealth and extreme poverty

There is no need for the extremes of rich and poor in our world. And before anyone thinks I'm going after them or their families, when I say *rich*, I mean the billionaires of the world. Why should anyone have so much money they could not possibly spend it? Oxfam suggests that extreme wealth is a sign of a failing economic system and a shrinking middle class.

3. Protect caregivers rights and secure living wages

I've outlined how important our care economy is and how little our care workers are valued. Legislating a universal living wage would ensure that women around the world can access financial stability. Government cash allowances to pay for care work could go a long way to alleviating poverty.

4. Give caregivers influence over policy decisions

There are enough old white cisgender men making decisions for the rest of the world. It's time to recognize those who keep our economy afloat (hint: it's the unpaid and underpaid care workers), and make sure they have a say in policy decisions.

5. Challenge harmful and sexist beliefs

We all have a role to play in this one. Calling out sexist beliefs and harmful norms can be as simple as making sure that the only woman in the work meeting isn't always the one taking notes, or distributing childcare pickups and drop-offs equally between both partners.

6. Value care in business policies

Flexible hours, remote work options, and paid leave are going to be top business priorities in the coming years. Organizations have a role to play in supporting their employees. Those companies that don't support these policies will see a mass exodus from a generation of workers who demand (and require) flexibility.[6]

When we think about policies, we need to critically look at political candidates' platforms and at who our partners are voting for. Our individual lifestyles are unlikely to influence broad-sweeping worldwide changes, but we can collectively elect people who advocate for financially feminist policies. The Pink Tax runs deep within our society—it is so much more than paying for an expensive razor. It represents the costs, multiplied over and over again, coming from all areas of our lives. Who we vote for determines how these disparities are addressed. As women, we have a responsibility to ensure we are entering partnerships with people who support the advancement of women in how they vote. It's a tough pill to swallow, but we can't expect more from our bosses or government than we do from our significant others.

25

NATIONAL INTERESTS

ABOLISHING THE Pink Tax means doing away with any laws, rules, societal expectations, and policies that force women into untenable situations. Many countries around the world still have legislation that is anti-woman and anti-feminist:

- 113 countries do not mandate equal pay for equal work—hello, wage gap.

- 104 countries restrict the types of jobs women can hold—that's 2.75 billion women worldwide who are more likely to hold lower-paying jobs because of legal infrastructure.

- 18 countries require women to have their husband's permission to work outside the home.[1]

Working conditions have to change to achieve global equality in the workforce. There are also financial laws that hurt women's banks accounts:

- 132 countries do not mandate retailers to provide information to credit bureaus, which impedes women from building their credit score and history.

- 75 countries restrict women's rights to own property.

- 41 countries have an earlier retirement age to receive a full pension for men than for women.

- 6 African countries have different rules to open bank accounts for women than men.[2]

Maternity and parental leave are vital to close the gender wage gap, and while many countries offer some sort of leave, we aren't where we need to be yet:

- 3 countries (the US, Papua New Guinea, and Suriname) do not have paid maternity leave.

- 156 countries do not have tax deductions for childcare payments.

- 147 countries do not have legal paid parental leave.

- 86 countries do not pay full wages during maternity leave.

- 12 countries do not have legally mandated paid maternity leave.[3]

These are just a few examples of how we continue to do a disservice to women on the global stage. It's not all bad though. As we saw earlier, there are great examples of countries advocating and legislating for women's equality.

One area where inequity could be addressed at a national level is mandated board quotas. Countries such as Italy, Israel, Norway, Spain, Finland, Iceland, France, Kenya, and Belgium, and the Canadian province of Quebec, all require representation on organizational boards to be composed of 30 to 50 percent women.[4] (Unfortunately these policies are structured on a false gender binary.) Sitting on a board is advantageous for many reasons, and board composition in the nonprofit sector is more equitable than in corporations. Paid public company boards are still dominated by older white cisgender men.

But you can't just throw your name in the hat to sit on a prestigious paid board at Apple or Coca-Cola. You need experience to sit on a board even at a much smaller company. To get experience, you need to sit on a few nonprofit boards and work your way up. Without gender mandates, boards appoint people who look the same as they do, with diversity considerations of all kinds left as an afterthought.

Board involvement bolsters a résumé and a personal brand. It allows people to expand their networks—think "It's not what you know, it's who you know"—and can make a person better at their current job. Men have these advantages—growing their networks, becoming better at their jobs, and building their personal brands—so it's no wonder we continue to see a wage gap.

Gender mandates force boards to find well-qualified women to fill board positions. And if you're one of those people who thinks that tokenism hurts women, and that companies should recruit the "best person for the job," I implore you to ask why, in a country such as Canada with 38 million people, or the US with 331 million, we cannot find a few qualified women to fit the role? This answer is that we aren't looking hard enough.

Mandating an end to the Pink Tax

Twelve countries around the world have been deemed to have appropriate laws protecting men and women equally. Countries were ranked across thirty-three indicators to calculate an equality score, and Belgium, Canada, Denmark, France, Greece, Iceland, Ireland, Latvia, Luxembourg, Portugal, Spain, and Sweden were deemed to have equal legal rights, obtaining a perfect score.[5]

There is still so much work to do when it comes to gender equality… but we don't have to look very far to find amazing examples of countries advancing gender equality every year. We don't have to reinvent the wheel: the research has been done, and existing policies have been rolled out in certain countries, which can be used to advance all societies.

National mandates for equal pay for equal work and maternity and parental leave policies allow women the same opportunities as men for promotions in the workforce. It was 1963 when employers in the US and Canada were required to pay women equally for jobs that required the same skill, effort, and responsibility.[6]

Sweden's 480 days of parental leave has a catch: dual income households get the full amount only if both parents take at least ninety days. This kind of stipulation normalizes men as caregivers.

Abolishing the Pink Tax **means doing away with any laws, rules, societal expectations, and policies that force women into untenable situations.**

Canada's $10 a day daycare plan will make quality care for children more affordable and potentially increase the number of women in the workforce—something desperately needed since a fifth of all working women left the workforce during the pandemic that began in 2020, a level of participation last seen in 1981.[7]

In Germany, if you work for a company of more than two hundred people, you have the legal right to find out the pay of your differently gendered colleagues. Wage transparency laws ensure companies are in compliance with equal pay for equal work.

Lastly, and by far my favorite, is the work that Iceland is doing. As of 2018, Iceland requires companies to prove equal pay in their financial disclosures, with daily fines if they fail to do so. Iceland is ranked first on the World Economic Forum's Global Gender Gap Index, identifying it as the country with the smallest gender wage gap.[8]

As a side note, beyond labor laws, countries can support the high cost of being a woman by ditching the tax on menstrual products (which Canada did in 2015) or offering free birth control to people under the age of twenty-five (as France has done). In the United Kingdom, the cost of an abortion is covered, and in Scotland, the Period Products Act provides free menstrual products. When we eliminate the added costs associated with being a woman, we will see women's discretionary income increase, getting us one step closer to closing the wealth gap.

It's about damn time.

26

ERASING BARRIERS

O NCE I was giving a client presentation, along with my team. I'd done this kind of presentation a zillion times and always received positive feedback, so I felt confident. But one of the client's represen- tatives, a man, interrupted me several times. Later I was taken off the account because, I was told, the client didn't feel I "gave off a traditional accountant vibe." A less experi- enced older white man replaced me. I am told he went on to present the same material, uninterrupted. What breaks my heart about this particular experience is not that I was interrupted but that my company's solution was to replace me, because the client didn't like the way I talked or looked. It felt like no one had my back.

I mention this as an example of the kind of insidious sexism that can affect the trajectory of women's careers and our earnings. Of course, it is all of our responsibility to advocate within our companies for appropriate support for women in the workforce. And it is the companies' respon- sibility to look past their biases, assess their cultures and policies, and implement progressive changes.

When we look at promotions from an organizational perspective, the data tells us organizations expect women to be more qualified than men for the same leadership opportunities. Men are also promoted for what they promise to do, whereas women have to demonstrate what they have accomplished. When men get promotions, they are supported with more resources than women.[1] Resources could be a variety of things but typically mean more training, bigger team budgets, and more administrative help. The cards are stacked to see men succeed in C-suite roles.

I found out I was pregnant right as I was up for a promotion. I didn't want to let my leadership team know I was pregnant because I wanted that promotion. Then the pandemic hit, and promotions for that year were pushed. I eventually had to tell them that I was pregnant and they promised me the promotion for 2021, while I was scheduled to be on leave. But to no one's surprise, I didn't get promoted in 2021 or in 2022 when I came back from my maternity leave. I was ignored. A performance review was not completed for me while I was on leave (even though I asked for one repeatedly), and when I tried to engage with the company during my fourteen-month leave to stay up-to-date on my career progression, I was told that the company couldn't speak to me while I was on leave and that I was given the same treatment as a cancer patient.

Being on maternity leave was bad for my bank account and my career, and coming back to work made me feel as if I was starting from square one. I would say having a baby was one of the worst decisions I could have made for my career. My fears had come true: I was experiencing the motherhood penalty, something I had tried so hard to avoid.

In the Fortune 500, only forty-four CEO roles are filled by women[2] and just two[3] of those women are Black. When women are brought into the C-suite, they often face what is commonly referred to as the *glass cliff*: a woman (or member of a minority) is given a leadership position under challenging circumstances and with a high risk of failure. Women are more likely to be promoted to a C-suite position when a company is facing a downturn or crisis. Glass cliff hires are made under the guise of turning the company around, but in reality the hires are doomed to fail based on the precarious state of the business.[4] Marissa Mayer, Meg Whitman, Mary Barra, and Irene Rosenfeld were all glass cliff hires at large public companies. Marissa Mayer was hired at Yahoo! only to learn the financial despair it was in—flat revenue year over year among other issues. Mary Barra, the CEO of General Motors, took on the role only to be faced with a slew of safety recalls that led to senate hearings. The examples go on and on.

Glass cliff hires are part of a larger bias that puts women in positions where they are less likely to succeed. If you're a woman brought in to solve a complex problem or save a company, ask for more resources and support. A man in your shoes would just be given them.

How companies can provide support

There are companies making positive strides toward supporting women in the workplace, and as we see more legislation to address bias, the compensation gap will close. However, that's just one facet. There are other things that companies can do to support women.

Women are more likely to be promoted to a C-suite position when a company is facing a downturn or crisis, commonly referred to as the *glass cliff*.

Onsite subsidized daycare would be an absolute game changer for working parents. This could save women an hour or more a day of rushing to and from daycare. They would be able to pop down and see their kids on a coffee break or lunch hour. Currently, only 6 percent[5] of companies offer any subsidized childcare, and it's incredibly challenging to find examples of onsite subsidized childcare available to parents in either Canada or the US.

Not only do women earn less once they become parents, it can be incredibly expensive for some to prolong their biological window or to get pregnant in the first place. Companies could offer egg freezing as part of their health benefits and cover (or reimburse) any egg freezing, in vitro, or surrogacy costs incurred, which the company HubSpot already does.

Once women who've had children return to work, companies could offer milk storage through companies like Milk Stork, as well as nursing/pumping rooms for moms who return to work while they are still breastfeeding. Companies need strong policies on maternity leave pay gap distributions; they need to understand how large these gaps are and take immediate steps to close them. After extended leaves, return to work programs are essential to making women feel supported and included. Companies such as Honeywell are leading the charge on this front, through buddy programs, training, and connecting with women while they are on leave.[6]

Companies must also offer flexible hours and paid maternity leave. In 2022, people should have the option to work remotely when their child has the day off school or is sick.

We need flexible work schedules, and the number of hours you sit at your desk shouldn't be the indicator of who works the hardest.

Lastly, let's all consider the distribution of office housework, or non-promotable tasks. Women usually end up planning parties and organizing charity events.[7] Those events are important, but when it comes time for performance reviews, rarely are those activities factored in when promotions and raises are on the table. If you enjoy doing those things, like I do, keep doing them, but do what you can to make sure a man is on the committee and doing the same amount of work as you are.

27

DIGITAL
INEQUALITIES

ONE OF the best ways that women can gain financial control is to get involved with their finances, early and often. It can feel overwhelming to start, but technology has democratized financial management and made it much simpler. Owning your financial future is more accessible and easier to navigate than ever before.

Technology in this context includes everything from online banking to bitcoin to an Apple Watch. Our entire financial world, from our banking systems to our supply chains, is built on technology. It's important to understand how you can leverage tech tools to make your financial life easier (such as by setting up automatic transfers like we talked about earlier).

But there is a darker side of technology that you need to be aware of, especially as it relates to machine learning and artificial intelligence. Bias is baked into a lot of algorithms because they were predominantly created by white cisgender men who did not factor in an awareness of difference. These algorithms leverage biased data. Take facial recognition, for example. There is a 34 percent error[1] in gender classification when Black women's photos are run through facial recognition software, with near 100 percent accuracy for white men. You have to be careful about how such biases might affect you and your wallet.

How might automated approvals for financial products be impacted by biases baked into technology? Could this mean higher mortgage rates or lower credit approvals for people of color and white women because the algorithm has been taught to behave a certain way? We must look at the systems, technology, and their influence in order to make changes in the financial technology space. Free courses such as Sarah Kaplan's on gender and the economy, offered through the Rotman School of Management at the University of Toronto, are a great way to learn about beating the bias in tech.

Technology can solve many of the world's problems if it is used correctly and put into the hands of the right people. The unbanked and underbanked are predominantly women. We can leverage technology to reduce some of the barriers to traditional banking. The unbanked typically have trouble setting up bank accounts for a variety of reasons; for instance, they may not have ID or a permanent address. But without a bank account, you may not be able to receive government benefits or sign up for certain services. Financial institutions like ATB Financial here in Alberta are allowing people that are unhoused and unbanked to set up bank accounts using fingerprint and facial recognition technology, giving them safety and security for their money. This is currently only available at one branch in Edmonton, but my hope is that they will roll it out across the province.

We could use retina scanning or thumbprint technology to create access to a bank account for those who don't have a permanent address or government-issued ID. This service could increase financial stability for many, which is good for the entire economy and leads to more positive outcomes in mental and physical health.

"We'll never solve the feminization of power until we solve the masculinity of wealth."

GLORIA STEINEM

THE FUTURE IS EQUAL

MONEY MAKES the world go round, which means women need to step into their power as we continue to increase the amount of wealth we control. Money is a top stressor for everyone, but women on average are less likely to be financially independent. Women aggregated across all racial groups still only hold $0.32 of wealth for every dollar a man owns,[1] while women of color own just $0.02.[2] We know that systemic bias against women drives this gap: it lessens our earnings, hits us again with the Pink Tax when we spend, and ultimately compounds when women invest less and with less confidence compared to men. The deck is stacked against us, but that doesn't make us powerless.

In the US, a third of women currently earn more than their husbands,[3] and more women than ever choose not to marry or enter into a long-term monogamous shared-resources relationship. With this turning tide, more women are learning about their money, talking to their friends about their financial struggles, and becoming more involved with building their wealth.

There is still a lot of work to be done as we build a society that supports financial feminism and smash the Pink Tax. Building wealth shouldn't be seen as greedy but as a way to achieve financial independence and build a dream life. It can give you the stability to choose if and how much you want to work and allow you to live a comfortable life in your later years. Everyone deserves to have this, and it shouldn't be a luxury. It should be table stakes in our society.

We can't continue to tell people to just "save more" or "work harder"—if it were that easy, I'd know a lot more billionaires. Yes, individuals do need to take steps to secure their financial futures, but we also have to address the macroeconomic side and create policies and laws that pay living wages and support people when they can't work. Your ability to put food on the table shouldn't be based on your employment status. Your worth as a human should not be tied to your bank account balance. And your access to medical and health related services shouldn't be dependent on your employer. We need to pay for the unpaid care work that our society has benefited from for hundreds of years, work that is predominantly done by women. And we need to require companies and governments to step up to support and empower women, so that we all benefit.

Let's build it together

Imagine a world in which women are paid the same as men. A world where we don't need to worry if we are being paid less than our colleagues because salary information is publicly available. Boards across the country are truly diverse in many ways, including gender.

In this world we are building, household chores are split fifty-fifty—meaning partners have equal time to pursue passions in addition to meaningful careers. You don't have to worry about being looked over for a promotion if you have a baby because it's commonplace for both parents to take time away from work when their child is born. When you come back to work, there is onsite daycare, subsidized by your company and the government, and you visit your little one on coffee breaks and lunch hour.

You have amassed a small nest egg, and you're investing in your future. You are confident enough to invest in the stock market, and you see upwards of 10 percent return on the money you've worked so hard to earn. You're financially secure and free to make the decisions that are important to you and your family without fear of financial hardship or repercussions.

Doesn't that sound like a pretty grand place to live?

It doesn't need to take 250 years or more to get there... Personally, I'd like to see us get there in my lifetime.

It's possible. All we have to do is smash the Pink Tax and embrace financial feminism.

ACKNOWLEDGMENTS

M Y LITTLEST baby bear, I started writing this book
when you were eight months grown in my womb.
You are my inspiration for making this world a
better, fairer, and more equal place. You are my
inspiration each day I wake up and get out of bed, and I
truly cannot even fathom what life was like before you.
Teddy, I love you.

To my mentors along the way, Lesley-Anne Scorgie,
Courtney Kirschbaum, Mandy Balak, Rachel Miller, Selina
Gray, and Jane Stoller—thank you for pushing and encouraging me to take the risks and make the big moves. This
book wouldn't have been possible without you.

My Heroic Public Speaking family, thank you for your
continual guidance in this industry and making me into a
referable speaker. Amy and Michael, it has been an absolute honor to by coached by you. AJ Harper, thank you for
giving me the confidence to write a book that wasn't in a
well-accepted genre by asking everyone on that eight-hour
writing sprint who would preorder my book. That was the
fuel I needed to get started, even though I was eight months

pregnant. Fotini and Robin, my HPS classmates, mentors, and now friends. Thank you for every conversation, piece of feedback, glass of wine, or city we have explored together. Oh, and thank you for pushing me in the right direction for the title of this book—I'm sure my publishers thank you too.

On that note, the team at Page Two, you have been an absolute delight to work with. Thank you Trena for seeing the vision of this book, Caela for managing this project beautifully, and Kendra for shaping this book. To everyone else who had a hand to play in *The Pink Tax*, thank you for all of the love and feminist passion you have put into it. I could not have picked a better, more aligned publisher.

To my community and everyone along the way who has supported me in any way, thank you. Whether it's purchasing something from my company, sharing my content, or simply just engaging with me online, I appreciate you. This book would not have been possible without all of you and your willingness to share your stories with me.

To Merv and Lori, the very best in-laws a girl could ask for—thank you for always supporting my dreams by helping with care for Theodore. There are no better grandparents (or in-laws) on the planet.

Papa and Donna, it is the most wonderful feeling to be able to share my successes and accomplishments with my grandparents—your encouragement and excitement means so much!

Mom and Dad, thank you for encouraging me to ask questions and to go after anything I want and for giving me the privilege to build wealth. I could not have written this book without the foundation you laid.

Jake, I am so glad I was connected to you years ago. Your work is so important in this fight to smash the patriarchy; you are an inspiration to me every day, probably more than you know. Thank you for your work.

Mark, to the man I mislabeled as a patriarchal Texas cowboy, I couldn't have been more wrong. You are the kindest and most genuine human I have ever met, and I'm so appreciative that we get to learn and discuss challenging topics together. You make me think in the best way possible, and many of these chapters were influenced by conversations we had.

To my biggest cheerleaders along the way, Janessa, Emma, Natasha, Aislin, and Tara.

Janessa, you are always the first person to jump on the like button or comment on a piece of content I put out—thank you, it means so much to always have your support and love.

Emma and Natasha, your unwavering compassion for all that I do does not go unnoticed. Thank you for cheering me on, celebrating all the things, while simultaneously bringing me back to earth in a grounded way. I care so much for both of you.

Aislin and Tara, you have challenged me to think in ways I didn't know possible—thank you for continuing to educate me and open my eyes.

Tara, your brilliance and your passion to build a better, more compassionate earth continue to motivate and empower me. Thank you for starting the podcast with me— we are chaotic in our conversations and I love it.

I am very lucky to have all you ladies in my corner.

Nothing can be done without the support of other humans around you, and whenever people ask how I do so much, I remember how lucky I am to have so much support in my corner. Aurora, Mary Joy, Erica, thank you for taking care of my baby, cleaning my house, and helping me with my business at various points throughout this process. Your kindness and willingness does not go unnoticed, and this book would not have been possible without you.

My therapist, Beth, thank you for the healing you have helped me with over the past number of years. Your willingness to understand, your patience, and the work you do with your patients to help them through their traumas are gifts to the world. I would not be in the position I am today without you.

Sissy (Julia), your humility and excellence in the practice of medicine encourages me to change lives in my own way (without any blood or guts, please). I am so proud of you and could not have written this book without your love and support. You are such a compassionate human, and I truly try to encompass the love you have for your patients in the work I do with people's money.

Lazer, my puppy, thank you for the cuddles when everything in the world seems way too hard. You are the best boy.

Steven—*cues the tears*—my best friend of fifteen years, my COO, my sounding board. What would I do without you? Thank you for literally being alive. For scribbling through the first pass of my manuscript during the three weeks you stayed with us in Calgary during the pandemic to take care of Theo. For scrambling to reference everything in a 150-page doc, due yesterday, while halfway around the world. For encouraging me to go get everything I've ever wanted and cheering me on along the way—I could not do it without you. I know we tell people we're siblings, but I am convinced at this point we are—my brother, I love you.

Andrew, the love of my life. You have been the source of my journey to understanding what feminism is for the past twelve years. I cannot believe my luck—picking you as a tutor off a UofA registry list. The world wasn't ready for us. You have and will always be my biggest supporter and most committed cheerleader, and I can't thank you enough. Thank you for being such an amazing partner, a true fifty-fifty; helping me find time to write this book; booking hotel rooms for writing retreats to get away from the chaos—while never ever making me feel any mom guilt. I really can't wait for the rest of our lives together. I know we're in for a wild, beautiful ride.

NOTES

Got the Pink Tax Blues?

1   Emily A. Shrider, Melissa Kollar, Frances Chen, and Jessica
    Semega, "Income and Poverty in the United States: 2020,"
    United States Census Bureau, report number P60-273,
    September 14, 2021, census.gov/library/publications/
    2021/demo/p60-273.html; Greg Daugherty, "Women Still
    Earn Less Than Men for Comparable Work in 2022 America,"
    Investopedia, updated May 25, 2022, investopedia.com/
    history-gender-wage-gap-america-5074898.

2   Spencer Feingold, "What Is the 'Pink Tax' and How Does
    It Hinder Women?" World Economic Forum, July 14, 2022,
    weforum.org/agenda/2022/07/what-is-the-pink-tax-and-
    how-does-it-hinder-women/.

3   Beth Dreher, "What Is the Pink Tax? If You're a Woman, It's
    Costing You Lots of Money Every Year," *Good Housekeeping*,
    May 23, 2019, goodhousekeeping.com/life/money/a27409442/
    what-is-pink-tax.

4   Ian Ayres and Peter Siegelman, "Race and Gender
    Discrimination in Bargaining for a New Car," *American
    Economic Review* 85, no. 3 (1995): 304–21, jstor.org/
    stable/2118176.

5   Catherine J. Nash, "Patriarchy," in *International Encyclopedia
    of Human Geography*, 2nd ed., edited by Audrey Kobayashi
    (Cambridge, MA: Elsevier, 2020), 43–47, doi.org/10.1016/
    B978-0-08-102295-5.10206-9.

6   "Feminism," *Merriam-Webster*, merriam-webster.com/dictionary/feminism.

7   Kara, "A Working Definition of Financial Feminism," Bravely Go, bravelygo.co/financial-feminism.

8   "Timeline: Women's Suffrage," *The Canadian Encyclopedia*, thecanadianencyclopedia.ca/en/timeline/womens-suffrage.

9   Ron Sanders, "The History of Women and Money in the United States in Honor of Women's History Month," ONE Advisory Partners (blog), March 7, 2017, oneadvisorypartners.com/blog/the-history-of-women-and-money-in-the-united-states-in-honor-of-womens-history-month.

10 LeBach Pham, "When Could Women Have a Bank Account? A Short History of Financial Gender Equality and the Financial Road Ahead," Spiral (blog), April 22, 2021, spiral.us/blog/when-could-women-have-a-bank-account-a-short-history-of-financial-gender-equality-and-the-financial-road-ahead.

11 John F. Leslie, "Indigenous Suffrage," *The Canadian Encyclopedia*, April 7, 2016, thecanadianencyclopedia.ca/en/article/indigenous-suffrage.

12 "Canadian Women's History," Public Service Alliance of Canada, January 9, 2013, psac-ncr.com/canadian-womens-history.

13 "Not All Women Gained the Vote in 1920," American Experience, PBS, July 6, 2020, pbs.org/wgbh/americanexperience/features/vote-not-all-women-gained-right-to-vote-in-1920.

14 "Key Findings," *Global Gender Gap Report 2020*, World Economic Forum, December 16, 2019, weforum.org/reports/gender-gap-2020-report-100-years-pay-equality/digest.

15 Elle Tibbitts and Becca Smith, "How Social Support Can Help Lower-Income People Save Money," Commonwealth (blog), April 1, 2021, buildcommonwealth.org/blog/how-social-support-can-help-lower-income-people-save-money.

16 "Meritocracy," *Merriam-Webster*, merriam-webster.com/dictionary/meritocracy.

17 "The History and Future of Meritocracy," *The Economist*, June 3, 2021, economist.com/books-and-arts/2021/06/03/the-history-and-future-of-meritocracy.

18 Roge Karma, "'The Meritocracy Trap,' Explained," Vox, October 24, 2019, vox.com/policy-and-politics/2019/10/24/20919030/meritocracy-book-daniel-markovits-inequality-rich.

19 Daniel Markovits, *The Meritocracy Trap: How America's Foundational Myth Feeds Inequality, Dismantles the Middle Class, and Devours the Elite* (New York: Penguin, 2019).

20 Mazamesso Assih, "Women's Financial Literary Benefits Us All—Here's How," World Economic Forum, February 24, 2022, weforum.org/agenda/2022/02/women-financial-literacy.

Part 1: Demand Financial Equality

1 Office of the Assistant Secretary for Administration & Management, "Equal Pay for Equal Work," US Department of Labor, dol.gov/agencies/oasam/centers-offices/civil-rights-center/internal/policies/equal-pay-for-equal-work.

2 "Facts: Gender Economic Inequality," Inequality.org, inequality.org/facts/gender-inequality/.

1. Through a New Lens

1 "Consumer Price Index, May 2022," Statistics Canada, June 22, 2022, www150.statcan.gc.ca/n1/daily-quotidien/220622/dq220622a-eng.htm.

2 Jane Thier, "The Cost of Childcare Has Risen by 41% during the Pandemic with Families Spending up to 20% of Their Salaries," *Fortune*, January 28, 2022, fortune.com/2022/01/28/the-cost-of-child-care-in-the-us-is-rising.

3 "Table 3: Average Daily Child Care Fees ($) per Child by Age Group and by Business Type, January 2020 and January 2021," Statistics Canada, June 15, 2021, www150.statcan.gc.ca/n1/daily-quotidien/210615/t003c-eng.htm.

4 "Student Debt Crisis—A Generation Buried in Student Debt," Joe Debtor Annual Bankruptcy Study, Hoyes, Michalos (blog), 2018, hoyes.com/press/joe-debtor/the-student-debtor.

5 "Canadian Housing Market News," WOWA Leads, last updated October 18, 2022, wowa.ca/reports/canada-housing-market.

6   Joni Sweet, "How U.S. Labor Productivity Has Changed since
    1950," Stacker, September 1, 2020, stacker.com/stories/4068/
    how-us-labor-productivity-has-changed-1950.

7   Greg Iacurci, "Women Are Still Paid 83 Cents for Every Dollar
    Men Earn. Here's Why," Empowered Investor (CNBC), May 19,
    2022, cnbc.com/2022/05/19/women-are-still-paid-83-cents-
    for-every-dollar-men-earn-heres-why.html.

8   Bonnie Chiu, "Invisibility of Race in Gender Pay Gap
    Discussions," Forbes, June 13, 2019, forbes.com/sites/
    bonniechiu/2019/06/13/invisibility-of-race-in-gender-pay-gap-
    discussions/?sh=4d2cc5ab5664.

9   "Distribution of Household Wealth in the U.S. since 1989,"
    Board of Governors of the Federal Reserve System, last
    updated September 23, 2022, federalreserve.gov/releases/
    z1/dataviz/dfa/distribute/table/#quarter:119;series:Net%20
    worth;demographic:generation;population:all;units:shares.

10 Hillary Hoffower, "Millennials Dominate the US
    Workforce, but They're Still 10 Times Poorer Than
    Boomers," Insider, October 12, 2020, businessinsider.com/
    millennials-versus-boomers-wealth-gap-2020-10.

11 Dean Baker, "Correction: The $23 an Hour Minimum Wage,"
    Center for Economic and Policy Research (blog), August 19,
    2021, cepr.net/the-26-an-hour-minimum-wage.

12 Laurie Monsebraaten, "Quebec's Child-Care Scheme Pays for
    Itself, Economist," Toronto Star, June 22, 2011, thestar.com/
    life/parent/2011/06/22/quebecs_childcare_scheme_pays_for_
    itself_economist.html; "Sweden—Parental Benefits and
    Benefits Related to Childbirth," European Commission,
    Employment, Social Affairs & Inclusion, ec.europa.eu/social/
    main.jsp?catId=1130&intPageId=4808&langId=en; "Equal Pay
    Certification," Government of Iceland, government.is/
    topics/human-rights-and-equality/equality/equal-pay-
    certification/; Jill Petzinger, "By Law, Women in Germany
    Can Now Find Out What Their Male Peers Are Earning," Quartz,
    January 5, 2018, qz.com/work/1171514/by-law-women-in-
    germany-can-now-find-out-what-their-male-peers-are-earning.

2. Take Back the Fight

1   Pooneh Baghai, Olivia Howard, Lakshmi Prakash, and
    Jill Zucker, "Women as the Next Wave of Growth in US
    Wealth Management," McKinsey & Company, July 29, 2020,
    mckinsey.com/industries/financial-services/our-insights/
    women-as-the-next-wave-of-growth-in-us-wealth-management.

2   Dana George, "3 Ways RBG Revolutionized Women's
    Finances," The Ascent, updated July 25, 2021, fool.com/
    the-ascent/personal-finance/articles/3-ways-rbg-revolutionized-
    womens-finances/.

3. The Value of Judgment-Free Cash

1   "Low Income Cut-Offs (LICOs) before and after Tax by
    Community Size and Family Size, in Current Dollars," Statistics
    Canada, Table 11-10-0241-01, released March 23, 2022,
    www150.statcan.gc.ca/t1/tbl1/en/tv.action?pid=1110024101
    &pick Members%5B0%5D= 2.2&cubeTimeFrame.startYear=
    2020&cubeTimeFrame.endYear=2020&referencePeriods=
    20200101%2C20200101.

2   Sigal Samuel, "When a California City Gave People a Guaranteed
    Income, They Worked More—Not Less," *Vox*, March 6, 2021,
    vox.com/future-perfect/22313272/stockton-basic-income-
    guaranteed-free-money; see also Annie Lowrey, *Give People
    Money: How a Universal Basic Income Would End Poverty,
    Revolutionize Work, and Remake the World* (New York: Crown,
    2018).

4. Payment Isn't Biased; the Payer Is

1   "Fair Banking," ACORN Canada, acorncanada.org/fair-banking.

2   "Women and Predatory Lending," ACORN Canada,
    acorncanada.org/resources/women-and-predatory-lending.

5. Cashless

1   ACORN Canada, submission to Bank Act review, canada.ca/
    content/dam/fin/migration/consultresp/pdf-pssge-psefc/
    pssge-psefc-03.pdf.

2   Luca Ventura, "World's Most Unbanked Countries 2021,"
    Global Finance, February 17, 2021, gfmag.com/global-data/
    economic-data/worlds-most-unbanked-countries.

3   Sean Cooper, "What Credit Score Do You Need for a
    Mortgage?" Borrowell, January 7, 2022, borrowell.com/blog/
    credit-score-mortgage-canada.

4   Amy Fontinelle, "The 5 Biggest Factors That Affect Your Credit,"
    Investopedia, updated May 21, 2021, investopedia.com/articles/
    pf/10/credit-score-factors.asp.

6. Smash Student Debt

1   "The Lifelong and Generational Benefits of an Educated
    Society," Restavek Freedom (blog), October 17, 2017,
    restavekfreedom.org/2018/10/17/the-lifelong-and-generational-
    benefits-of-an-educated-society.

2   "Student Debt from All Sources, by Province of Study and Level
    of Study," Statistics Canada, Table 37-10-0036-01, released
    November 5, 2019, doi.org/10.25318/3710003601-eng.

3   Melanie Hanson, "Student Loan Debt Statistics," Education Data
    Initiative, last updated October 26, 2022, educationdata.org/
    student-loan-debt-statistics.

4   "Student Debt Crisis," Joe Debtor Annual Bankruptcy Study,
    Hoyes, Michalos.

5   "Why Do Women Hold the Most Student Debt?" Her First
    $100K (blog), March 22, 2022, herfirst100k.com/blog-posts/
    women-student-debt.

6   Oliver McNeil, "The Burden of LGBTQ Student Loan Debt,"
    Center for LGBTQ Economic Advancement & Research,
    November 19, 2020, lgbtq-economics.org/2020/11/19/
    the-burden-of-lgbtq-student-loan-debt.

7   National Student Loans Service Centre (NSLSC), "Enhancing
    the Repayment Assistance Plan," last modified October 3, 2022,
    csnpe-nslsc.canada.ca/en/home.

8   "Jagmeet Singh Commits to Cancelling Up to $20,000 Per
    Person in Federal Student Loan Debt," NDP, March 20, 2021,
    ndp.ca/news/jagmeet-singh-commits-cancelling-20-000-
    person-federal-student-loan-debt; Zack Friedman, "Student

Loan Forgiveness: New Blockbuster Plan to Cancel
Student Loans," *Forbes*, August 5, 2022, forbes.com/sites/
zackfriedman/2022/08/05/student-loan-forgiveness-
republicans-propose-blockbuster-plan-to-cancel-student-loans.

7. Out-Waged

1   Leila Schochet, "The Child Care Crisis Is Keeping Women
    Out of the Workforce," Center for American Progress,
    March 28, 2019, americanprogress.org/article/child-care-
    crisis-keeping-women-workforce.

2   Susan Colantuono, "The Career Advice You Probably Didn't
    Get," TEDxBeaconStreet, September 30, 2014, ted.com/talks/
    susan_colantuono_the_career_advice_you_probably_didn_t_get.

3   Tara Sophia Mohr, "Why Women Don't Apply for Jobs
    Unless They're 100% Qualified," *Harvard Business Review*,
    August 25, 2014, hbr.org/2014/08/why-women-dont-apply-
    for-jobs-unless-theyre-100-qualified.

4   Margaretta Midura, "John vs. Jennifer: A Battle of the Sexes,"
    Yale Scientific, February 19, 2013, yalescientific.org/2013/02/
    john-vs-jennifer-a-battle-of-the-sexes.

5   The Economist Intelligence Unit, "The New Face of Wealth
    and Legacy: How Women Are Redefining Wealth, Giving
    and Legacy Planning," RBC Wealth Management, 2018,
    https://www.rbcwealthmanagement.com/en-us/insights/
    the-new-face-of-wealth-and-legacy-how-women-are-
    redefining-wealth-giving-and-legacy-planning.

6   Becky Little, "When Computer Coding Was a 'Woman's' Job,"
    History.com, updated February 9, 2021, history.com/news/
    coding-used-to-be-a-womans-job-so-it-was-paid-less-and-
    undervalued.

7   Patrick Boyle, "Nation's Physician Workforce Evolves:
    More Women, a Bit Older, and toward Different Specialties,"
    Association of American Medical Colleges, February 2, 2021,
    aamc.org/news-insights/nation-s-physician-workforce-
    evolves-more-women-bit-older-and-toward-different-
    specialties.

8   Christina Loguidice, "Pediatricians Continue to Be Lowest
    Paid Physicians: Is the Specialty in Peril?" *Physician's Weekly*,
    October 13, 2021, physiciansweekly.com/pediatricians-
    continue-to-be-lowest-paid-physicians-is-the-specialty-in-peril.

8. Perpetuating the Gap

1   Oxfam International, "Extreme Inequality and Essential
    Services," oxfam.org/en/what-we-do/issues/extreme-
    inequality-and-essential-services.

2   Lawrence Mishel and Julia Wolfe, "CEO Compensation Has
    Grown 940% since 1978," Economic Policy Institute, August 14,
    2019, epi.org/publication/ceo-compensation-2018/.

3   Emma Hinchliffe, "The Female CEOs on This Year's Fortune
    500 Just Broke Three All-Time Records," *Fortune*, June 2, 2021,
    fortune.com/2021/06/02/female-ceos-fortune-500-2021-
    women-ceo-list-roz-brewer-walgreens-karen-lynch-cvs-
    thasunda-brown-duckett-tiaa/.

4   Ronny Reyes, "The New Gilded Age: Top 0.01% of Wealthiest
    Individuals Now Hold 11% of the World's Wealth—Up More
    Than $400bn from 10% in 2020—While 100 Million Fell
    in to Extreme Poverty," *Daily Mail*, December 7, 2021,
    dailymail.co.uk/news/article-10284667/Top-0-01-wealthy-
    individuals-hold-11-worlds-wealth-10-2020.html.

5   Charles Riley, "22 Men Own More Wealth Than Africa's 326
    Million Women, Oxfam Says," CNN Business, January 20, 2020,
    cnn.com/2020/01/19/business/oxfam-billionaires/index.html.

6   Mikel Jollett, "Ok how about this…" @Mikel_Jollett, Twitter
    post, March 22, 2020, twitter.com/mikel_jollett/status/
    1241843944238923777?lang=en.

7   Katie Warren, "Jeff Bezos Is the First Person Ever to Be Worth
    $200 Billion. This Is How the Amazon CEO's Immense Wealth
    Stacks Up to the Average US Worker, the British Monarchy,
    and Entire Countries' GDP," *Insider*, October 21, 2020,
    businessinsider.com/how-rich-is-jeff-bezos-mind-blowing-
    facts-net-worth-2019-4.

8   Hiatt Woods, "How Billionaires Saw Their Net Worth
     Increase by Half a Trillion Dollars during the Pandemic,"
     Insider, October 30, 2020, businessinsider.com/billionaires-
     net-worth-increases-coronavirus-pandemic-2020-7.
9   "Not All Gaps Are Created Equal: The True Value of Care Work,"
     Oxfam International, oxfam.org/en/not-all-gaps-are-created-
     equal-true-value-care-work.

Part 2: Build Wealth for Self-Care

1   "Self-Care Added to the Dictionary," PAGB, September 27, 2017,
     pagb.co.uk/latest-news/self-care-added-dictionary.
2   "Canadians and Their Money: Key Findings from the 2019
     Canadian Financial Capability Survey," Financial Consumer
     Agency of Canada, Government of Canada, updated December
     20, 2021, canada.ca/en/financial-consumer-agency/programs/
     research/canadian-financial-capability-survey-2019.html.
3   Sarah Foster, "Survey: More Than Half of Americans Couldn't
     Cover Three Months of Expenses with an Emergency Fund,"
     Bankrate, July 21, 2021, bankrate.com/banking/savings/
     emergency-savings-survey-july-2021.

9. Financial Feelings

1   Rosanne S. DeTorres, "Is It Worth Staying in a Marriage
     Financial Reasons?" DeTorres & DeGeorge, January 18, 2022,
     danddfamilylaw.com/is-it-worth-staying-in-a-marriage-
     financial-reasons/.
2   Jessica Mai, "5 Ways Women Are Better with Money Than
     Men," *Insider*, March 7, 2016, businessinsider.com/ways-
     women-are-better-with-money-2016-3.
3   Christy Bieber, "5 Quotes That Will Make You Rethink Your
     Personal Finances," The Motley Fool, November 2, 2019,
     fool.com/personal-finance/2019/11/02/5-quotes-that-will-
     make-you-rethink-your-personal.aspx.

10. Lattes and Lies

1   Anne Boden, "Why We Need to #MakeMoneyEqual,"
    Starling Bank, March 13, 2018, starlingbank.com/blog/
    make-money-equal.

2   David Bach, *The Automatic Millionaire: A Powerful One-Step Plan
    to Live and Finish Rich* (New York: Broadway Books, 2004).

11. The Pain of Payment

1   "Why Do We Think Less about Some Purchases Than
    Others?" The Decision Lab, thedecisionlab.com/biases/
    mental-accounting.

2   Trevor Wheelwright, "2022 Cell Phone Usage Statistics:
    How Obsessed Are We?" Reviews.org, January 24, 2022,
    reviews.org/mobile/cell-phone-addiction.

12. Patriarchy-Proof Finances

1   Maurie Backman, "Women and Investing: 20 Years of Research
    and Statistics Summarized," The Motley Fool, updated March 9,
    2022, fool.com/research/women-in-investing-research.

2   "Canada Inflation Rate," Trading Economics,
    tradingeconomics.com/canada/inflation-cpi.

3   "The Toronto-Dominion Bank (TD)," Yahoo! Finance,
    finance.yahoo.com/quote/TD/financials.

4   Dave Ramsey, "If you're working on paying off debt..."
    @DaveRamsey, Twitter post, February 17, 2020, twitter.com/
    DaveRamsey/status/1229425772546449409.

5   Samantha Emann, "'I'm Begging All of You': Suze Orman Says
    Avoid These 5 Financial Missteps If You Are Trying to Climb Out
    of Debt," *MoneyWise*, updated September 13, 2022, yahoo.com/
    now/dont-afraid-no-suze-orman-110000442.html.

6   Eva M. Krockow, "How Many Decisions Do We Make Each Day?"
    Psychology Today, September 27, 2018, psychologytoday.com/
    ca/blog/stretching-theory/201809/how-many-decisions-do-we-
    make-each-day.

7   "Survey: Millennials Experience Financial Stress, the Majority
    Ignore It to Cope," MintLife (blog), updated July 26, 2022,
    mint.intuit.com/blog/personal-finance/financial-stress-survey.

8   Jaanika Meriküll, Merike Kukk, and Tairi Rõõm, "What Explains
    the Gender Gap in Wealth? Evidence from Administrative
    Data," *Review of Economics of the Household* 19 (2021): 501–47,
    doi.org/10.1007/s11150-020-09522-x.

13. Take Back the Bank

1   Marie-Claire Chappet, "Why Don't Women Ask for Professional
    Help When It Comes to Our Finances?" *Glamour*, September
    19, 2020, glamourmagazine.co.uk/article/financial-advice-
    women; Robbie Lawther, "Third of Female Advice Clients Feel
    Patronised," *International Adviser*, May 2, 2019, international-
    adviser.com/third-of-female-advice-clients-feel-patronised.
2   Mark Murphy, "Neuroscience Explains Why You Need to Write
    Down Your Goals If You Actually Want to Achieve Them," *Forbes*,
    April 15, 2018, forbes.com/sites/markmurphy/2018/04/15/
    neuroscience-explains-why-you-need-to-write-down-your-goals-
    if-you-actually-want-to-achieve-them.

14. Disaster-Proof Your Finances

1   Katie Porter, "Women. Accounted. For. All. The. Losses."
    @katieporteroc, Twitter post, January 8, 2021, twitter.com/
    katieporteroc/status/1347685399020277761.
2   "COVID-19 and Its Economic Toll on Women: The Story
    behind the Numbers," UN Women, September 16, 2020,
    unwomen.org/en/news/stories/2020/9/feature-covid-19-
    economic-impacts-on-women.
3   Kristen Doerer, "How Much Does It Cost to Leave the
    Workforce to Care for a Child? A Lot More Than You Think,"
    PBS *NewsHour*, June 21, 2016, pbs.org/newshour/economy/
    how-much-does-it-cost-to-leave-the-workforce-to-care-for-
    a-child-a-lot-more-than-you-think.
4   Canadian Women's Foundation, "The Facts: Women and
    Pandemics," last updated October 2022, canadianwomen.org/
    the-facts/women-and-pandemics.
5   Elsie Boskamp, "60+ Incredible Diversity in the Workplace
    Statistics: Facts You Need to Know," Zippia, July 7, 2022,
    zippia.com/advice/diversity-in-the-workplace-statistics.

6   "The Shadow Pandemic: Violence against Women during
    COVID-19," UN Women, May 27, 2020, unwomen.org/en/
    news/in-focus/in-focus-gender-equality-in-covid-19-response/
    violence-against-women-during-covid-19.

7   Erica Alini, "Over Half of Canadians Are $200 or Less Away
    from Not Being Able to Pay Bills," Global News, May 8, 2017,
    globalnews.ca/news/3434447/over-half-of-canadians-are-200-
    or-less-away-from-not-being-able-to-pay-bills/.

8   Rob Carrick, "We All Just Schooled by Rogers on the
    Importance of Having Cash on Hand," *Globe and Mail*,
    July 11, 2022, theglobeandmail.com/investing/personal-
    finance/article-rogers-outage-internac-cash.

15. Money Mindsets and Mantras

1   Trauma of Money, thetraumaofmoney.com.

2   Beth Kobliner, "Money Habits Are Set by Age 7. Teach Your
    Kids the Value of a Dollar Now," PBS *NewsHour*, April 5, 2018,
    pbs.org/newshour/economy/making-sense/money-habits-are-
    set-by-age-7-teach-your-kids-the-value-of-a-dollar-now.

3   Theodora Blanchfield, "How to Shift from a Scarcity Mindset
    to an Abundance Mindset," Verywell Mind, March 24, 2022,
    verywellmind.com/how-to-shift-from-a-scarcity-mindset-to-
    an-abundance-mindset-5220862.

16. Ask for More

1   Kim Elsesser, "Why Women Fall Short in Negotiations
    (It's Not Lack of Skill)," *Forbes*, January 21, 2021, forbes.com/
    sites/kimelsesser/2021/01/21/why-women-fall-short-in-
    negotiations-its-not-lack-of-skill.

2   Carol Sankar, "Why Don't More Women Negotiate?" *Forbes*,
    July 13, 2017, forbes.com/sites/forbescoachescouncil/2017/
    07/13/why-dont-more-women-negotiate.

3   Julia Pollak, "The ZipRecruiter 2018 Annual Job Seeker Survey:
    Economic Security & Opportunity—Job Seekers' Perceptions
    10 Years after the Financial Crisis," ZipRecruiter (blog),
    December 13, 2018, ziprecruiter.com/blog/ziprecruiter-2018-
    annual-job-seeker-survey/.

4   Fotini Iconomopoulos, *Say Less, Get More: Unconventional Negotiation Techniques to Get What You Want* (Toronto: Collins, 2021).

17. Financial Confidence

1   Tabea Bucher-Koenen, Rob Alessie, Annamaria Lusardi, and Maarten van Rooij, "Fearless Woman: Financial Literacy and Stock Market Participation," Global Financial Literacy Excellence Center, March 2021, gflec.org/wp-content/uploads/2021/03/Fearless-Woman-Research-March-2021.pdf.
2   Samantha Fields, "States Are Adding a New Requirement for High School Graduation: Financial Literary," *Marketplace Morning Report*, June 9, 2022, marketplace.org/2022/06/09/states-are-adding-a-new-requirement-for-high-school-graduation-financial-literacy.

18. Internalized Capitalism

1   Cathy Ching, "Work Hard, Work Harder: The Uproar of Internalized Capitalism in the Digital World," *Huntington News* (Northeastern University), December 29, 2021, huntnewsnu.com/67424/campus/work-hard-work-harder-the-uproar-of-internalized-capitalism-in-the-digital-world.
2   Caroline Castrillon, "Why Companies Should Consider a Four-Day Workweek," *Forbes*, October 17, 2021, forbes.com/sites/carolinecastrillon/2021/10/17/why-companies-should-consider-a-four-day-workweek/?sh=19be14d23b45.

19. Wealth Becomes Her

1   Capital Group, *Women Investors: A Powerful and Confident, Yet Often Misunderstood, Economic Force*, Wisdom of Experience Investor Survey Series, October 2017, capitalgroup.com/content/dam/cgc/tenants/capgroup/documents/02_CR_PR%20WOE%20Part%202%20Women%20REPORT.pdf.
2   Brad M. Barber and Terrance Odean, "Boys Will Be Boys: Gender, Overconfidence, and Common Stock Investment," *Quarterly Journal of Economics* 116, no. 1 (2001): 261–92, doi.org/10.1162/003355301556400.

3   Maurie Backman, "Women and Investing: Key Findings and
    Opportunities," Fidelity Investments, March 9, 2022, fidelity.ca/
    en/investor/investorinsights/womenandinvesting.
4   Ann Senne, "As Women Gain Power, Interest in ESG Investing
    Grows," RBC Wealth Management, March 8, 2021,
    https://www.rbcwealthmanagement.com/en-us/insights/
    as-women-gain-power-interest-in-esg-investing-grows.
5   Preet Banerjee, "Mutual Fund Fees over 25 Years … Ouch," Bonds
    Are for Losers, December 19, 2011, bondsareforlosers.com/
    detailed-breakdown-of-the-real-impact-of-mers-on-an-
    investment-portfolio-over-time.

20. Worth Less

1   "Why 80% of Women Leave Their Advisors When They
    Lose Their Husband," Advisorpedia, March 15, 2017,
    advisorpedia.com/advisor-tools/why-80-of-women-leave-
    their-advisors-when-they-lose-their-husband.
2   Barbara Stewart, "Suddenly Single: How to Plan with
    Female Clients," CFA Institute (blog), October 18, 2019,
    blogs.cfainstitute.org/investor/2019/10/18/suddenly-single-
    how-to-plan-with-female-clients.
3   R.J. Shook, "Women Feel Ignored by Advisors, Study Says,"
    Forbes, August 7, 2020, forbes.com/sites/rjshook/2020/08/07/
    woman-feel-ignored-by-advisors-study-says.
4   Anna Zakrzewski et al., "Managing the Next Decade of
    Women's Wealth," Boston Consulting Group, April 9, 2020,
    bcg.com/publications/2020/managing-next-decade-
    women-wealth.

Part 3: Support New Mothers

1   Denise Comanne, "How Patriarchy and Capitalism Combine
    to Aggravate the Oppression of Women," Committee for the
    Abolition of Illegitimate Debt, May 28, 2020, cadtm.org/
    How-Patriarchy-and-Capitalism-Combine-to-Aggravate-the-
    Oppression-of-Women.

21. Affordable, Accessible Childcare Is a Must

1   Ben Franklin and Dean Hochlaf, "Women in the Labour Market: Boosting Mothers' Employment and Earnings through Accessible Childcare," Centre for Progressive Policy, October 14, 2021, progressive-policy.net/publications/women-in-the-labour-market-2.

2   "Nearly 350 Million Children Lack Quality Childcare in the World," The World Bank (press release), March 4, 2021, https://www.worldbank.org/en/news/press-release/2021/03/04/nearly-350-million-children-lack-quality-childcare-in-the-world.

3   Ruba Hassan, "Fees Are Dropping! See How Much Less Child Care Could Cost in Your City," *Today's Parent,* May 10, 2022, todaysparent.com/kids/daycare/fees-are-dropping-see-how-much-less-child-care-could-cost-in-your-city.

4   Vinusha Gunaseelan, "A New Normal for Child Care in Canada: Accessible, Affordable, Universal," Wellesley Institute, January 27, 2021, wellesleyinstitute.com/children-youth/a-new-normal-for-child-care-in-canada-affordable-accessible-universal.

5   "Child Care Costs vs. Income," Quicken (blog), December 21, 2015, quicken.com/blog/child-care-costs-vs-income/; Kabir Agarwal, "Parental Benefits around the World in 5 Infographics," *ReThink Quarterly* 6 (ADP), September 15, 2022, rethinkq.adp.com/parental-benefits-global-infographics.

6   David Macdonald, *Child Care Deserts in Canada,* Canadian Centre for Policy Alternatives, June 28, 2018, policyalternatives.ca/publications/reports/child-care-deserts-canada.

7   "Population Replacement Rate," Energy Education, n.d., energyeducation.ca/encyclopedia/Population_replacement_rate.

22. Parental Leave Penalties

1   "C003—Maternity Protection Convention, 1919 (No. 3)," International Labour Organization, adopted November 29, 1919, ilo.org/dyn/normlex/en/f?p=NORMLEXPUB:12100:0::NO::P12100_INSTRUMENT_ID:312148.

2   "More Than 120 Nations Provide Paid Maternity Leave,"
    International Labour Organization (press release), February
    16, 1998, ilo.org/global/about-the-ilo/newsroom/news/
    WCMS_008009/lang--en/index.htm.

3   Erin Eatough, "What Is Mental Load? Recognize the Burden of
    Invisible Labor," BetterUp (blog), January 4, 2022, betterup.com/
    blog/mental-load.

4   Michelle J. Budig, "The Fatherhood Bonus and the Motherhood
    Penalty: Parenthood and the Gender Gap in Pay," Third
    Way, September 2, 2014, https://www.thirdway.org/report/
    the-fatherhood-bonus-and-the-motherhood-penalty-
    parenthood-and-the-gender-gap-in-pay.

5   "How Big Is the Wage Penalty for Mothers?" *The Economist*,
    January 28, 2019, economist.com/graphic-detail/2019/01/28/
    how-big-is-the-wage-penalty-for-mothers.

6   Ava Wardecki, "The Motherhood Penalty," Global Women (blog),
    March 8, 2021, globalwomen.org.nz/news/motherhood-penalty.

7   Shelley J. Correll, Stephen Benard, and In Paik, "Getting a Job: Is
    There a Motherhood Penalty?" *American Journal of Sociology* 112,
    no. 5 (2007): 1297–339, doi.org/10.1086/511799.

8   Anne-Marie Slaughter, *Unfinished Business: Women Men Work
    Family* (New York: Random House, 2015).

9   "More Than 120 Nations Provide Paid Maternity Leave."

10 Janna van Belle, *Paternity and Parental Leave Policies across the
    European Union*, RAND Europe, 2016, rand.org/pubs/research_
    reports/RR1666.html.

11 van Belle, *Paternity and Parental Leave Policies across the
    European Union.*

12 N. van der Gaag et al., *State of the World's Fathers:
    Unlocking the Power of Men's Care* (Washington, DC:
    Promundo–US), 2019, stateoftheworldsfathers.org/report/
    state-of-the-worlds-fathers-helping-men-step-up-to-care.

23. For Richer or Poorer

1   Sasha-Ann Simons, "More Couples Are Embracing
    Female Breadwinners, Despite Decades-Old Stigma,"
    WAMU 88.5 (NPR), February 18, 2020, npr.org/
    local/305/2020/02/18/807050015/more-couples-are-
    embracing-female-breadwinners-despite-decades-old-stigma.

2   "Not All Gaps Are Created Equal: The True Value
    of Care Work," Oxfam International, oxfam.org/en/
    not-all-gaps-are-created-equal-true-value-care-work.

3   Stephanie Convery and Luke Henriques-Gomes, "Women
    Do 21 Hours More Unpaid Work Than Men a Week,
    National Survey Finds," *The Guardian*, December 6, 2021,
    theguardian.com/australia-news/2021/dec/07/women-do-21-
    hours-more-unpaid-work-than-men-study-suggests.

4   "How Much Is a Mom Really Worth? The Amount May Surprise
    You," Salary.com, n.d., salary.com/articles/how-much-is-a-
    mom-really-worth -the-amount-may-surprise-you.

5   "Thousands Risk Pension Poverty after Divorce," Aviva
    (press release), May 3, 2022, aviva.com/newsroom/news-
    releases/2022/05/thousands-risk-pension-poverty-
    after-divorce.

6   Leslie Silva, "The Socio-Economic Division among Women in
    Child Support Proceedings," American Bar Association,
    June 18, 2021, americanbar.org/groups/litigation/committees/
    woman-advocate/practice/2021/the-socio-economic-division-
    among-women-in-child-support-proceedings.

7   Silva, "The Socio-Economic Division among Women";
    United States Census Bureau, "44 Percent of Custodial Parents
    Receive the Full Amount of Child Support"
    (press release), January 30, 2018, census.gov/newsroom/
    press-releases/2018/cb18-tps03.html.

8   Terri Huggins, "Millennials: Financially Confident but Very
    Stressed," Investopedia, updated September 5, 2022,
    investopedia.com/millennials-are-financially-confident-but-
    stressed-5224413.

9   Nicholas Vega, "Nearly 40% of Couples Who Live Together
    Don't Know How Much Their Partner Makes—
    Experts Say That's a Problem," Make It (CNBC), July 15, 2021,
    cnbc.com/2021/07/15/40-percent-of-couples-who-live-
    together-dont-know-how-much-partner-makes.html.

10 Jasmin Suknanan, "54% of People Believe a Partner with
    Debt Is a Reason to Consider Divorce—Here Are
    Other Ways Debt May Affect Your Marriage," Select
    (CNBC), updated December 20, 2022, cnbc.com/select/
    national-debt-relief-survey-debt-reason-for-divorce.

11 Suknanan, "54% of People Believe a Partner with Debt."

12 "Divorce Statistics: Over 115 Studies, Facts and Rates for
    2022," Wilkinson & Finkbeiner (blog), wf-lawyers.com/
    divorce-statistics-and-facts.

13 "Kids, Allowance and Gender," Anti-Defamation League,
    September 14, 2018, adl.org/education/resources/
    tools-and-strategies/kids-allowance-and-gender.

14 "What Is Financial Abuse?" Women's Aid, womensaid.org.uk/
    information-support/what-is-domestic-abuse/financial-abuse.

15 Sharon Epperson and Stephanie Dhue, "How These Couples
    Overcame Financial Infidelity, Money Secrets in Their
    Relationships," Invest in You (CNBC), February 11, 2022,
    cnbc.com/2022/02/11/how-couples-overcame-financial-
    infidelity-money-secrets-.html.

16 "Financial Abuse Fact Sheet," National Network to End
    Domestic Violence, nnedv.org/wp-content/uploads/2019/07/
    Library_EJ_Financial_Abuse_Fact_Sheet.pdf.

17 Adam Jacobs, "5 Common Signs of Financial Abuse," Legal
    Aid DC, October 19, 2021, makingjusticereal.org/5-common-
    signs-of-financial-abuse.

24. No Justice without Gender Justice

1   "Gender Budgeting: Checklist for Putting the Horizontal
    Principle of Gender Equality into Practice in Operational
    Programmes," European Institute for Gender Equality,
    eige.europa.eu/gender-mainstreaming/toolkits/

gender-budgeting/checklist-putting-horizontal-principle-gender-equality-practice-operational-programmes.

2   *OECD Toolkit for Mainstreaming and Implementing Gender Equality: Implementing the 2015 OECD Recommendation on Gender Equality in Public Life*, OECD, 2018, oecd.org/gov/toolkit-for-mainstreaming-and-implementing-gender-equality.pdf.

3   Alejandro Hoyos Guerrero, Karla Dominguez Gonzalez, and Cecilia Escalante Hernandez, "Women Pay More: The Additional Costs Faced by Female Transport Users," World Bank (blog), March 25, 2021, blogs.worldbank.org/transport/women-pay-more-additional-costs-faced-female-transport-users.

4   "Gender Impact Assessment: Belgium," European Institute for Gender Equality, eige.europa.eu/gender-mainstreaming/toolkits/gender-impact-assessment/belgium.

5   International Institute for Democracy and Electoral Assistance, "Country Data: Portugal," Gender Quota Database, updated June 14, 2022, idea.int/data-tools/data/gender-quotas/country-view/247/35.

6   Max Lawson et al., *Time to Care: Unpaid and Underpaid Care Work and the Global Inequality Crisis*, Oxfam International, January 20, 2020, oxfam.org/en/research/time-care.

25. National Interests

1   "Women's Workplace Equality Index," Council on Foreign Relations, cfr.org/legal-barriers.

2   "Women's Workplace Equality Index."

3   "Women's Workplace Equality Index."

4   Siri Terjesen, Ruth V. Aguilera, and Ruth Lorenz, "Legislating a Woman's Seat on the Board: Institutional Factors Driving Gender Quotas for Boards of Directors," *Journal of Business Ethics* 50, no. 2 (2015): 233–51, doi.org/10.1007/s10551-014-2083-1.

5   World Bank, *Women, Business and the Law 2022* (Washington, DC: World Bank, 2022), doi.org/10.1596/978-1-4648-1817-2.

6   Amy Fontinelle, "Equal Pay Act of 1963," Investopedia, updated November 29, 2022, investopedia.com/equal-pay-act-1963-5207271.

7   Jamie Orsini, "New Report: 1 in 5 Women Have Left the Workforce since the Pandemic Began," Motherly, December 14, 2020, mother.ly/career-money/work-and-motherhood/women-in-the-workforce.

8   World Economic Forum, *Global Gender Gap Report 2022: Insight Report, July 2022*, www3.weforum.org/docs/WEF_GGGR_2022.pdf.

26. Erasing Barriers

1   Herminia Ibarra, Nancy M. Carter, and Christine Silva, "Why Men Still Get More Promotions Than Women," Harvard Business Review, September 2010, hbr.org/2010/09/why-men-still-get-more-promotions-than-women.

2   Morgan Smith, "3 Fortune 500 CEOs Share the Advice, Lessons and Skills That Have Shaped Their Success," Make It (CNBC), July 22, 2022, cnbc.com/2022/07/22/fortune-500-ceo-roz-brewer-kathy-warden-beth-ford-best-career-advice.html.

3   Jasmine Browley, "Two Black Women CEOS Make History on Fortune 500 List," *Essence*, June 7, 2021, essence.com/news/money-career/two-black-women-ceos-make-history-on-fortune-500-list.

4   Kelly Oakes, "The Invisible Danger of the 'Glass Cliff,'" BBC Future, February 6, 2022, bbc.com/future/article/20220204-the-danger-of-the-glass-cliff-for-women-and-people-of-colour.

5   Terri Williams, "Report: Only 6% of US Companies Offer Comprehensive Child Care Benefits," MultiBriefs, February 27, 2020, exclusive.multibriefs.com/content/report-only-6-of-us-companies-offer-comprehensive-child-care-benefits/business-management-services-risk-management.

6   "Honeywell Initiatives Offer Support for Women Returners after Career Breaks Like Honeywell India's Return to Work Program and Competitive Maternity Leave," Where Women Work, wherewomenwork.com/Career/1427/Honeywell-women-returners.

7   Alison Green, "My Office Sticks Women with All the Party Planning," *Inc.*, September 9, 2019, inc.com/alison-green/my-office-sticks-women-with-all-party-planning.html.

27. Digital Inequalities

1   Alex Najibi, "Racial Discrimination in Face Recognition Technology," *Science in the News* (blog), Harvard University, October 24, 2020, sitn.hms.harvard.edu/flash/2020/racial-discrimination-in-face-recognition-technology.

The Future Is Equal

1   Colleen Briggs and Heather McCulloch, "Closing the Women's Wealth Gap," JPMorgan Chase & Co. (blog), March 28, 2018, jpmorganchase.com/news-stories/cbriggs-closing-the-womens-wealth-gap.

2   Mariko Chang, *Women and Wealth: Insights for Grantmakers*, Asset Funders Network, 2015, static1.squarespace.com/static/5c50b84131d4df5265e7392d/t/5c54781a8165f5b854 6f8a34/1549039642955/AFN_Women_and_Wealth_Brief_2015. pdf; Heather McCulloch, *Closing the Women's Wealth Gap: What It Is, Why It Matters, and What Can Be Done about It*, Closing the Women's Wealth Gap (CWWG) initiative, updated January 2017, womenswealthgap.org/wp-content/uploads/2017/06/Closing-the-Womens-Wealth-Gap-Report-Jan2017.pdf.

3   Nihal Krishan, "Wives Now Out-Earn Their Husbands Nearly a Third of the Time," *Washington Examiner*, February 1, 2020, washingtonexaminer.com/policy/economy/wives-now-out-earn-their-husbands-nearly-a-third-of-the-time.

ABOUT THE AUTHOR

JANINE ROGAN, CPA, is a passionate keynote and TEDx speaker. She is the founder and CEO of The Wealth Building Academy Inc. and an award-winning CPA. Her mission is to educate and empower women to confidently and profitably grow their wealth, through financial equality for all.

She has been featured in international media (BNN, Yahoo! Finance, CTV, and more) and has delivered keynotes to thousands of individuals and companies around the world. She currently sits on the CPA Alberta Education Foundation board, the board of the Further Education Society of Alberta (FESA), and the planning committee of the AICPA Women's Global Leadership Summit. She is also the cohost of the *Pink Tax Podcast*—where she and Tara Faria smash the patriarchy one dollar at a time.

Janine is a University of Alberta alumna, born and raised in Edmonton, Canada, and is currently pursuing her Master of Economics of Sustainability at Torrens University in Adelaide, Australia. She lives in Calgary with her husband, Andrew, and their son, Theodore.

ENGAGE WITH ME!

I HAVE A GREAT LIST of resources online to help you learn more about the topics covered in this book. I'm constantly updating it with new resources, authors, and organizations, including suggestions from readers. There is no registration or password required, and I think you'll be impressed.

Visit anytime at **pinktaxbook.com/resources**.

INTERESTED IN GIVING *The Pink Tax* to your management team or organization?

Contact me at **hello@janinerogan.com** to arrange a bulk order of the print, ebook, or audiobook editions.